S0-BYE-064

Catholic Book
of
PRAYERS

Jesus said: "Let your focus be on the Kingdom of God and His justice, and all these things will be given to you as well."

Catholic Book
of
PRAYERS

POPULAR CATHOLIC PRAYERS
ARRANGED FOR EVERYDAY USE

IN LARGE PRINT

Edited by

REV. MAURUS FITZGERALD, O.F.M.

Illustrated

CATHOLIC BOOK PUBLISHING CORP.
NEW JERSEY

NIHIL OBSTAT: Daniel V. Flynn, J.C.D.
Censor Librorum

IMPRIMATUR: Joseph T. O'Keefe
Vicar General, Archdiocese of New York

(T-910)

www.catholicbookpublishing.com

Printed in Korea

CONTENTS

FOREWORD

THIS new large-type Prayer Book has been edited in strict accordance with the mind of the Church which considers the Liturgy as the "summit toward which the activity of the Church is directed, and at the same time the fountain from which all her power flows."

However, the Church also declares that "the spiritual life is not limited solely to participation in the Liturgy. The Christian is indeed called to pray with his brethren, but he must also enter into his chamber to pray to the Father in secret. . . . Popular devotions of the Christian people are to be highly commended, provided they accord with the laws and norms of the Church. . . .

"But these devotions should be so drawn up that they harmonize with the liturgical seasons, accord with the sacred Liturgy, are in some fashion derived from it, and lead the people to it, since, in fact, the Liturgy by its very nature far surpasses any of them" (Vatican II: *Constitution on the Sacred Liturgy,* nos. 10, 12-13).

The present book has been inspired by these considerations and this spirit. It is based on the Liturgy with the Eucharist as its center since "in the divine Sacrifice of the Eucharist the entire work of our redemption is exercised" (Ibid., no. 2).

This book will help in disposing us to receive the Sacraments and to be united with God in the various circumstances of daily life, in times of trial and sorrow, and in the celebrations of the mysteries of salvation during the Liturgical Year.

Finally, it provides private devotions in honor of the Blessed Mother and the Saints which are intended to lead us to God, the Source of holiness and Giver of every good gift.

Rev. Maurus Fitzgerald, O.F.M.

COMMON PRAYERS

PRAYER is the path by which we can enter into intimate communion with God our Father, with Jesus, and with the Holy Spirit, our soul's most kindly Guest. By means of prayer we also communicate with Mary, the Mother of Jesus and our Mother as well, and with all the Saints in heaven together with whom we form one single Body, one single Church, whose Head is Christ.

We have constant need of prayer, therefore, in the same way that we need air to breathe. Prayer holds the key to our true happiness, our perseverance in faith and grace, our strength to avoid falling into sin, and our willingness to bear the weight of sorrows and trials. In a word, prayer holds the key to our eternal salvation.

Jesus bade us to pray always. We can put this divine command into action by living constantly in a state of love and adoration toward God, offering Him all our actions and especially our sufferings, seeking to carry out His will by observing the Commandments and the Gospel.

However, we must also dedicate a few moments of the day exclusively to the Lord, when by entering into intimate communion with Him by means of vocal or mental prayer on the things of God (for example, the Eucharist, and the Passion and Death of Christ) we can obtain the strength needed for our Christian life.

The Sign of the Cross

IN the name of the Father, and of the Son, ✠ and of the Holy Spirit. Amen.

The Lord's Prayer

OUR Father Who art in heaven, hallowed be Thy name; Thy kingdom come; Thy will be done on earth as it is in heaven. Give us this day our daily bread; and forgive us our trespasses as we forgive those who trespass against us; and lead us not into temptation, but deliver us from evil. Amen.

The Hail Mary

HAIL, Mary, full of grace! The Lord is with thee; blessed art thou among women, and blessed is the fruit of thy womb, Jesus. Holy Mary, Mother of God, pray for us sinners now and at the hour of our death. Amen.

Glory Be to the Father

GLORY be to the Father, and to the Son, and to the Holy Spirit. As is was in the beginning, is now, and will be forever. Amen.

The Apostles' Creed

I BELIEVE in God, the Father Almighty, Creator of heaven and earth; and in Jesus Christ, His only Son, Our Lord; Who was conceived by the Holy Spirit, born of the Virgin Mary, suffered under Pontius Pilate, was crucified, died and was buried. He descended into hell; the third day He arose again from the dead; He ascended into heaven, sitteth at the right hand of God, the Father Almighty; from thence He shall come to judge the living and the dead.

I believe in the Holy Spirit, the Holy Catholic Church, the communion of saints, the forgiveness of sins, the resurrection of the body, and life everlasting. Amen.

(This is the traditional version of the Apostles' Creed; the newer version is found on p. 50.)

The Confiteor

I CONFESS to Almighty God, to blessed Mary ever Virgin, to blessed Michael the Archangel, to blessed John the Baptist, to the holy Apostles Peter and Paul, and to all the saints, that I have sinned exceedingly in thought, word and deed, through my fault, through my fault, through my most grievous fault. Therefore, I beseech blessed Mary ever Virgin, blessed Michael the Archangel, blessed John the Baptist, the holy Apostles Peter and Paul, and all the saints, to pray to the Lord our God for me.

May Almighty God have mercy on me, forgive me my sins, and bring me to everlasting life. Amen.

May the almighty and merciful Lord grant me pardon, absolution, and remission of all my sins. Amen.

An Act of Faith

O MY God, I firmly believe that You are one God in three Divine Persons, Father, Son, and Holy Spirit; I believe that Your Divine Son became Man, and died for our sins, and that He will come to judge the living and the dead. I believe these and all the truths which the Holy Catholic Church teaches because You have revealed them, Who can neither deceive nor be deceived.

An Act of Hope

O MY God, relying on Your almighty power and infinite mercy and promises, I hope to obtain pardon for my sins, the help of Your grace, and life everlasting, through the merits of Jesus Christ, my Lord and Redeemer.

An Act of Love

O MY God, I love You above all things with my whole heart and soul, because You are all-good and worthy of all love. I love my neighbor as myself for the love of You. I forgive all who have injured me, and ask pardon of all whom I have injured.

Act of Contrition

O MY God, I am heartily sorry for having offended You, and I detest all my sins because of Your just punishments, but most of all because they offend You, my God, Who are all-good and deserving of all my love. I firmly resolve, with the help of Your grace, to sin no more and to avoid the unnecessary occasions of sin. Amen.

Prayer to the Holy Spirit

COME, Holy Spirit, fill the hearts of Your faithful and kindle in them the fire of Your love.

℣. Send forth Your Spirit, and they shall be created.

℟. **And You shall renew the face of the earth.**

Let us pray. O God, Who did instruct the hearts of the faithful by the light of the Holy Spirit: grant that, by the gift of the same Spirit, we may be always truly wise, and ever rejoice in His consolation. Through Christ our Lord. Amen.

The Angelus

℣. The Angel of the Lord declared unto Mary.

℟. **And she conceived of the Holy Spirit.**

Hail Mary, etc.

℣. Behold the handmaid of the Lord.

℟. **Be it done unto me according to Your word.**

Hail Mary, etc.

℣. And the Word was made flesh.

℟. **And dwelt among us.**

Hail Mary, etc.

℣. Pray for us, O holy Mother of God.

℟. **That we may be made worthy of the promises of Christ.**

Let us pray. Pour forth, we beseech You, O Lord, Your grace into our hearts, that we to whom the Incarnation of Christ, Your Son, was made known by the message of an angel, may by His Passion and Cross be brought to the glory of His Resurrection, through the same Christ our Lord. Amen.

Regina Caeli

(Said during Eastertide instead of the Angelus)

QUEEN of heaven, rejoice, alleluia. For He Whom you merited to bear, alleluia. Has risen as He said, alleluia. Pray for us to God, alleluia.

℣. Rejoice and be glad, O Virgin Mary, alleluia.

℟. **Because the Lord is truly risen, alleluia.**

Let us pray. O God, Who by the Resurrection of Your Son, our Lord Jesus Christ, granted joy to the whole world, grant, we beg You, that, through the intercession of the Virgin Mary, His Mother, we may attain the joys of eternal life. Through the same Christ our Lord. Amen.

Hail, Holy Queen

HAIL, Holy Queen, Mother of mercy, hail, our life, our sweetness, and our hope! To you do we cry, poor banished children of Eve! To you do we send up our sighs, mourning, and weeping in this vale of tears!

Turn then, most gracious advocate, your eyes of mercy toward us; and after this, our exile, show unto us the blessed fruit of your womb, Jesus! O clement, O loving, O sweet Virgin Mary!

Blessing before Meals

✠ Bless us, O Lord, and these Your gifts, which we are about to receive from Your bounty, through Christ our Lord. Amen.

Grace after Meals

✠ We give You thanks for all Your benefits, O Almighty God, Who live and reign forever. Amen.

May the souls of the faithful departed, through the mercy of God, rest in peace. Amen.

Act of Spiritual Communion

MY Jesus, I believe that You are in the Blessed Sacrament. I love You above all things, and I long for You in my soul. Since I cannot now receive You sacramentally, come at least spiritually into my heart. I know You have already come. I embrace You and unite myself entirely to You; never permit me to be separated from You.

DAILY PRAYERS

MORNING PRAYERS

Offering to the Holy Trinity

MOST holy and adorable Trinity, one God in three Persons, I praise You and give You thanks for all the favors You have bestowed upon me. Your goodness has preserved me until now. I offer You my whole being and in particular all my thoughts, words and deeds, together with all the trials I may undergo this day.

Give them Your blessing. May Your Divine Love animate them and may they serve Your greater glory.

I make this morning offering in union with the Divine intentions of Jesus Christ Who offers himself daily in the holy Sacrifice of the Mass, and in union with Mary, His Virgin Mother and our Mother, who was always the faithful handmaid of the Lord.

Glory be to the Father, and to the Son, and to the Holy Spirit. Amen.

For Divine Guidance through the Day

LORD, God Almighty, You have brought us safely to the beginning of this day. Defend us today by Your mighty power, that we may not fall into any sin, but that all our words may so proceed and all our thoughts and actions be so directed, as to be always just in your sight. Through Christ our Lord. Amen.

Direct, we beg You, O Lord, our actions by Your holy inspirations, and carry them on by Your gracious assistance, that every prayer and work of ours may begin always with You, and through You be happily ended. Amen.

Morning Offering

O MY God, I offer You all my prayers, works, and sufferings, in union with the Sacred Heart of Jesus, for the intentions for which He pleads and offers Himself in the Holy Sacrifice of the Mass, in thanksgiving for

Your favors, in reparation for my offenses, and in humble supplication for my temporal and eternal welfare, for the conversion of sinners, and for the relief of the poor souls in purgatory.

I wish to gain all the indulgences attached to the prayers I shall say and to the good works I shall perform this day.

Another Morning Offering

O JESUS, through the Immaculate Heart of Mary, I offer You my prayers, works, joys and sufferings of this day for all the intentions of Your Sacred Heart, in union with the Holy Sacrifice of the Mass throughout the world, in reparation for my sins, for the intentions of all our associates and in particular for all the intentions of this month (*mention intention if known*).

Prayer for God's Protection and Christ's Presence

AS I arise today,
may the strength of God pilot me,
the power of God uphold me,
the wisdom of God guide me.
May the eye of God look before me,
the ear of God hear me,
the word of God speak for me.
May the hand of God protect me,
the way of God lie before me,
the shield of God defend me,
the host of God save me.
May Christ shield me today . . .
Christ with me, Christ before me,
Christ behind me,

Christ in me, Christ beneath me,
Christ above me,
Christ on my right, Christ on my left,
Christ when I lie down, Christ when I sit,
Christ when I stand,
Christ in the heart of everyone who thinks of me,
Christ in the mouth of everyone who speaks of me,
Christ in every eye that sees me,
Christ in every ear that hears me.

(St. Patrick)

MIDAFTERNOON PRAYER

O DIVINE Savior, I transport myself in spirit to Mount Calvary to ask pardon for my sins, for it was because of humankind's sins that You chose to offer Yourself in sacrifice. I thank You for Your extraordinary generosity and I am also grateful to You for making me a child of Mary, Your Mother.

Blessed Mother, take me under your protection. St. John, you took Mary under your care. Teach me true devotion to Mary, the Mother of God. May the Father, the Son, and the Holy Spirit be glorified in all places through the Immaculate Virgin Mary.

INVOCATIONS

May the Holy Trinity be blessed.

Christ conquers!
Christ reigns!
Christ commands!

O Heart of Jesus,
burning with love for us,
inflame our hearts with love for You.

O Heart of Jesus,
I place my trust in You.
O Heart of Jesus,
all for You.

Most Sacred Heart of Jesus,
have mercy on us.
Teach me to do Your will,
because You are my God.
(Psalm 143:10)

Most Sacred Heart of Jesus,
have mercy on us.

O Lord,
increase our faith. *(Luke 17:5)*

Sweet Heart of Mary,
be my salvation.

Jesus, meek and humble of heart,
make my heart like unto Thine.

May the Most Blessed Sacrament
be praised and adored forever.

Pray for us, O Holy Mother of God,
that we may be made worthy of the promises of Christ.

Father, into Your hands
I commend my spirit.

(Luke 23:46; see Psalm 31:6)

Merciful Lord Jesus,
grant them everlasting peace.

Queen conceived without original sin,
pray for us.

Holy Mother of God, Mary ever Virgin,
intercede for us.

Holy Mary,
pray for us.

My Jesus,
mercy.

EVENING PRAYERS

Prayer to the Blessed Trinity

I ADORE You, my God, and I thank You for having created me, for having made me a Christian and preserved me this day. I love You with all my heart and I am sorry for having sinned against You, because You are infinite Love and infinite Goodness. Protect me during my rest and may Your love be always with me. Amen.

The Annunciation of the Blessed Virgin Mary — "The angel Gabriel was sent by God . . . to a virgin. . . . The angel came to her and said, 'Hail, full of grace!' " — *Lk 1:26-28.*

The Visitation of the Blessed Virgin Mary — "When Elizabeth heard Mary's greeting. . . . [she] exclaimed . . .: 'Blessed are you among women, and blessed is the fruit of your womb' " — *Lk 1:41f.*

The Birth of Our Lord Jesus Christ — Mary "gave birth to her first-born Son. She wrapped Him in swaddling clothes and laid him in a manger, because there was no room for them in the inn . . . " — *Lk 2:7.*

The Baptism of Our Lord Jesus Christ — "He beheld the Spirit of God descending like a dove and alighting on Him. And a voice came from the heaven, saying, 'This is My beloved Son.' "— *Mt 3:16f.*

Eternal Father, I offer You the Precious Blood of Jesus Christ in atonement for my sins and for all the intentions of our Holy Church.

Holy Spirit, Love of the Father and the Son, purify my heart and fill it with the fire of Your Love, so that I may be a chaste Temple of the Holy Trinity and be always pleasing to You in all things. Amen.

Plea for Divine Help

HEAR us, Lord, holy Father, almighty and eternal God; and graciously send Your holy angel from heaven to watch over, to cherish, to protect, to abide with, and to defend all who dwell in this house. Through Christ our Lord. Amen.

Prayer to Jesus

JESUS Christ, my God, I adore You and I thank You for the many favors You have bestowed on me this day. I offer You my sleep and all the moments of this night, and I pray You to preserve me from sin. Therefore, I place myself in Your most sacred Side, and under the mantle of our Blessed Lady, my Mother. May the holy angels assist me and keep me in peace, and may Your blessing be upon me.

Prayer for the Home

WE beseech You, O Lord, to visit this home, and to drive far from it all the snares of the enemy: let Your holy angels dwell therein so as to preserve us in peace; and let your blessing be always upon us. Through Christ our Lord. Amen.

Prayer to the Guardian Angel

ANGEL of God, my guardian dear, to whom His love entrusts me here, ever this night be at my side, to light and guard, to rule and guide. Amen.

Invocation to Jesus, Mary, and Joseph

JESUS, Mary, Joseph, I give You my heart and my soul. Jesus, Mary, Joseph, assist me in my last agony. Jesus, Mary, Joseph, may I sleep and rest in peace with You.

JESUS INSTITUTES THE HOLY EUCHARIST

HOLY MASS

"AT the Last Supper, on the night when He was betrayed, our Savior instituted the Eucharistic sacrifice of His Body and Blood. He did this in order to perpetuate the sacrifice of the Cross throughout the centuries until He should come again, and so to entrust to His beloved Spouse, the Church, a memorial of His Death and Resurrection: a sacrament of love, a sign of unity, a bond of charity, a Paschal banquet in which Christ is eaten, the mind is filled with grace, and a pledge of future glory is given to us" (Vatican II: *Sacred Liturgy,* no. 47).

Thus the Mass is:

1) the true *sacrifice* of the New Covenant, in which a holy and living Victim is offered, Jesus Christ, and we in union with Him, as a gift of love and obedience to the Father;

2) a *sacred meal* and *spiritual banquet* of the children of God;

3) a *Paschal meal,* which evokes the passage (passover) of Jesus from this world to the Father; it renders Him present and makes Him live again in souls, and it anticipates our definitive passage to the Kingdom of God;

4) a *communitarian meal,* that is, a gathering together of the Head and His members, of Jesus and His Church, His Mystical Body, in order to carry out a perfect divine worship.

Thus, the Mass is the greatest prayer we have. Through it we give thanks and praise to the Father for the wonderful future He has given us in His Son. We also ask forgiveness for our sins and beg the Father's blessing upon ourselves and our fellow human beings.

THE ORDER OF MASS

THE INTRODUCTORY RITES

Acts of prayer and penitence prepare us to meet Christ as he comes in Word and Sacrament. We gather in worship to celebrate our unity with him and with one another in faith.

STAND

Mass begins with an entrance procession of the ministers to the sanctuary, during which a chant is sung or the Entrance Antiphon of the day is recited.

GREETING (3 forms)

Priest: In the name of the Father, and of the Son, and of the Holy Spirit.

People: **Amen.**

(a)

Priest: The grace of our Lord Jesus Christ,
and the love of God,
and the communion of the Holy Spirit
be with you all.

People: **And with your spirit.**

(b) ———

Priest: Grace to you and peace from God our Father
and the Lord Jesus Christ.

People: **And with your spirit.**

(c) ———

Priest: The Lord be with you.

People: **And with your spirit.**

THE PENITENTIAL ACT (3 forms)

Priest: Brethren (brothers and sisters), let us acknowledge our sins,
and so prepare ourselves to celebrate the sacred mysteries.

(a) ———

Priest and People:

I confess to almighty God,
and to you, my brothers and sisters,
that I have greatly sinned,
in my thoughts and in my words,

in what I have done and in what I have failed to do;

And, striking their breast, they say:

through my fault, through my fault,
through my most grievous fault;

Then they continue:

therefore I ask blessed Mary ever-Virgin,
all the Angels and Saints,
and you, my brothers and sisters,
to pray for me to the Lord our God.

(b) ———

Priest: Have mercy on us, O Lord.

People: **For we have sinned against you.**

Priest: Show us, O Lord, your mercy.

People: **And grant us your salvation.**

(c)

Priest or other minister:
You were sent to heal the contrite of heart:
Lord, have mercy.

People: **Lord, have mercy.**

Priest or other minister:
You came to call sinners:
Christ, have mercy.

People: **Christ, have mercy.**

Priest or other minister:
You are seated at the right hand of the Father to intercede for us:
Lord, have mercy.

People: **Lord, have mercy.**

(Other invocations may be used.)

Absolution

At the end of any of the forms of the Penitential Act:

Priest: May almighty God have mercy on us,

forgive us our sins,
and bring us to everlasting life.
People: **Amen.**

KYRIE

Unless included in the Penitential Act, the Kyrie is sung or said by all, with alternating parts for the choir or cantor and for the people.

℣. Lord, have mercy.
℟. **Lord, have mercy.**
℣. Christ, have mercy.
℟. **Christ, have mercy.**
℣. Lord, have mercy.
℟. **Lord, have mercy.**

GLORIA

As the Church assembled in the Spirit, we praise and pray to the Father and the Lamb.

GLORY to God in the highest, and on earth peace to people of good will.

**We praise you,
we bless you,
we adore you,
we glorify you,**

we give you thanks for your great glory,
Lord God, heavenly King,
O God, almighty Father.

Lord Jesus Christ, Only Begotten Son,
Lord God, Lamb of God, Son of the Father,
you take away the sins of the world,
have mercy on us;
you take away the sins of the world,
receive our prayer;
you are seated at the right hand of the Father,
have mercy on us.

For you alone are the Holy One,
you alone are the Lord,
you alone are the Most High,
Jesus Christ,
with the Holy Spirit,
in the glory of God the Father.
Amen.

COLLECT

Priest: Let us pray.

The Priest and people pray silently for a while. Then the Priest says the Collect, which gives the theme of the particular celebration and asks God to help us. He concludes with the words:

. . . for ever and ever.

People: **Amen.**

THE LITURGY OF THE WORD

The proclamation of God's Word is always centered on Christ, present through his Word. Old Testament writings prepare for him; New Testament books speak of him directly. All of scripture calls us to believe once more and to follow. After the reading we reflect upon God's words and respond to them.

SIT

READINGS AND RESPONSORIAL PSALM

At the end of the first reading:

Reader: The word of the Lord.

People: **Thanks be to God.**

The people repeat the response sung by the cantor the first time and then after each verse.

At the end of the second reading:

Reader: The word of the Lord.

People: **Thanks be to God.**

ALLELUIA (Gospel Acclamation)

STAND

The people repeat the Alleluia after the cantor's Alleluia and then after the verse.

During Lent one of the following invocations is used as a response instead of the Alleluia:

(1) Glory and praise to you, Lord Jesus Christ!

(2) Glory to you, Lord Jesus Christ, Wisdom of God the Father!

(3) Glory to you, Word of God, Lord Jesus Christ!

(4) Glory to you, Lord Jesus Christ, Son of the Living God!

(5) Praise and honor to you, Lord Jesus Christ!

(6) Praise to you, Lord Jesus Christ, King of endless glory!

(7) Marvelous and great are your works, O Lord!

(8) Salvation, glory, and power to the Lord Jesus Christ!

GOSPEL

Deacon (or Priest): The Lord be with you.

People: **And with your spirit.**

Deacon (or Priest):

✠ A reading from the holy Gospel according to N.

People: **Glory to you, O Lord.**

At the end:

Deacon (or Priest): The Gospel of the Lord.

People: **Praise to you, Lord Jesus Christ.**

SIT

HOMILY

God's Word is spoken again in the Homily. The Holy Spirit speaking through the lips of the preacher explains and applies today's biblical readings to the needs of this particular congregation. He calls us to respond to Christ through the life we lead.

PROFESSION OF FAITH (CREED)

As a people we express our acceptance of God's message in the Scriptures and the Homily. We summarize our faith by proclaiming a creed handed down from the early Church.

All say the Profession of Faith on Sundays.

THE NICENE CREED

STAND

I believe in one God
the Father almighty,
maker of heaven and earth,
of all things visible and invisible.

I believe in one Lord Jesus Christ,
the Only Begotten Son of God,
born of the Father before all ages.
God from God, Light from Light,
true God from true God,
begotten, not made, consubstantial
with the Father;
through him all things were made.
For us men and for our salvation
he came down from heaven,

At the words that follow, up to and including **and became man,** ***all bow.***

and by the Holy Spirit was incarnate of the Virgin Mary,
and became man.

For our sake he was crucified under Pontius Pilate,
he suffered death and was buried,
and rose again on the third day
in accordance with the Scriptures.
He ascended into heaven
and is seated at the right hand of the Father.
He will come again in glory
to judge the living and the dead
and his kingdom will have no end.

I believe in the Holy Spirit, the Lord, the giver of life,
who proceeds from the Father and the Son,
who with the Father and the Son is adored and glorified,
who has spoken through the prophets.

I believe in one, holy, catholic and apostolic Church.
I confess one Baptism for the forgiveness of sins
and I look forward to the resurrection of the dead
and the life of the world to come. Amen.

OR:

THE APOSTLES' CREED

I believe in God,
the Father almighty,
Creator of heaven and earth,
and in Jesus Christ, his only Son, our Lord,

At the words that follow, up to and including the Virgin Mary, *all bow.*

who was conceived by the Holy Spirit,
born of the Virgin Mary,
suffered under Pontius Pilate,
was crucified, died and was buried;

he descended into hell;
on the third day he rose again from the dead;
he ascended into heaven,
and is seated at the right hand of God the Father almighty;
from there he will come to judge the living and the dead.

I believe in the Holy Spirit,
the holy catholic Church,
the communion of saints,
the forgiveness of sins,
the resurrection of the body,
and life everlasting. Amen.

THE UNIVERSAL PRAYER

(Prayer of the Faithful)

As a priestly people we unite with one another to pray for today's needs in the Church and the world.

After the Priest's introduction the Deacon or other minister sings or says the invocations.

People: **Lord, hear our prayer.**

(or other response, according to local custom)

At the end the Priest says the concluding prayer:

People: **Amen.**

THE LITURGY OF THE EUCHARIST

Made ready by reflection on God's Word, we enter now into the eucharistic sacrifice itself, the Supper of the Lord. We celebrate the memorial which the Lord instituted at his Last Supper. We are God's new people, the redeemed brothers and sisters of Christ, gathered by him around his table. We are here to bless God and to receive the gift of Jesus' Body and Blood so that our faith and life may be transformed.

PREPARATION OF THE GIFTS

SIT

The bread and wine for the Eucharist, with our gifts for the Church and the poor, are gathered and brought to the altar. We prepare our hearts by song or in silence as the Lord's table is being set.

PREPARATION OF THE BREAD

Blessed are you, Lord God of all creation,
for through your goodness we have received
the bread we offer you:
fruit of the earth and work of human hands,

it will become for us the bread of life.

If there is no singing, the Priest may say this prayer aloud, and the people reply:

People: **Blessed be God for ever.**

PREPARATION OF THE WINE

By the mystery of this water and wine
may we come to share in the divinity of Christ
who humbled himself to share in our humanity.
Blessed are you, Lord God of all creation,
for through your goodness we have received
the wine we offer you:
fruit of the vine and work of human hands,
it will become our spiritual drink.

If there is no singing, the Priest may say this prayer aloud, and the people reply:

People: **Blessed be God for ever.**

INVITATION TO PRAYER

Priest: Pray, brethren (brothers and sisters),
that my sacrifice and yours
may be acceptable to God,
the almighty Father.

STAND

People: **May the Lord accept the sacrifice at your hands**
for the praise and glory of his name,
for our good
and the good of all his holy Church.

The Priest, speaking in our name, says the Prayer over the Offerings, asking the Father to bless and accept these offerings.

People: **Amen.**

EUCHARISTIC PRAYER

We begin the eucharistic service of praise and thanksgiving, the center of the entire celebration, the central prayer of worship. We lift our hearts to God, and offer praise and thanks as the Priest addresses this prayer to the Father

through Jesus Christ. Together we join Christ in his sacrifice, celebrating his memorial in the holy meal and acknowledging with him the wonderful works of God in our lives.

Priest: The Lord be with you.

People: **And with your spirit.**

Priest: Lift up your hearts.

People: **We lift them up to the Lord.**

Priest: Let us give thanks to the Lord our God.

People: **It is right and just.**

The Priest says the Preface here.

HOLY, HOLY, HOLY

Priest and People:

Holy, Holy, Holy Lord God of hosts.
Heaven and earth are full of your glory.
Hosanna in the highest.
Blessed is he who comes in the name of the Lord.
Hosanna in the highest.

MEMORIAL ACCLAMATION

Priest: The mystery of faith.

People:

A. **We proclaim your Death, O Lord,**
and profess your Resurrection
until you come again.

B. **When we eat this Bread and drink this Cup,**
we proclaim your Death, O Lord,
until you come again.

C. **Save us, Savior of the world,**
for by your Cross and Resurrection
you have set us free.

GREAT AMEN

Priest: . . . for ever and ever.

People: **Amen.**

THE COMMUNION RITE

To prepare for the paschal meal, to welcome the Lord, we pray for forgiveness and exchange a sign of peace. Before eating Christ's Body and drinking his Blood, we must be one with him.

STAND

THE LORD'S PRAYER

The Priest asks the people to join him in the prayer that Jesus taught us.

Priest and People:

OUR Father, who art in heaven,
hallowed be thy name;
thy kingdom come,
thy will be done
on earth as it is in heaven.
Give us this day our daily bread,
and forgive us our trespasses,
as we forgive those who trespass against us;
and lead us not into temptation,
but deliver us from evil.

Priest: Deliver us, Lord, we pray,
from every evil,
graciously grant peace in our days,
that, by the help of your mercy,
we may be always free from sin
and safe from all distress,
as we await the blessed hope
and the coming of our Savior,
Jesus Christ.

People: **For the kingdom,**
the power and the glory are yours
now and for ever.

SIGN OF PEACE

The Priest says the prayer for peace:

LORD Jesus Christ,
who said to your Apostles:
Peace I leave you, my peace I give you,
look not on our sins,
but on the faith of your Church,

and graciously grant her peace and unity
in accordance with your will.
Who live and reign for ever and ever.

People: **Amen.**

Priest: The peace of the Lord be with you always.

People: **And with your spirit.**

Deacon (or Priest):
Let us offer each other the sign of peace.

The people exchange a sign of peace and charity, according to local custom.

LAMB OF GOD

Then the Priest takes the host, breaks it over the paten, and places a small piece in the chalice, saying quietly:

May this mingling of the Body and Blood
of our Lord Jesus Christ
bring eternal life to us who receive it.

Meanwhile the following is sung or said:

Lamb of God, you take away the sins of the world,
have mercy on us.
Lamb of God, you take away the sins of the world,
have mercy on us.
Lamb of God, you take away the sins of the world,
grant us peace.

The invocation may even be repeated several times if the breaking of the bread is prolonged. Only the final time, however, is **grant us peace** ***said.***

KNEEL

The Priest prays quietly before Communion.

INVITATION TO COMMUNION

The Priest genuflects, takes the host and, holding it slightly raised above the paten or above the chalice, while facing the people, says aloud:

Priest: Behold the Lamb of God, behold him who takes away the sins of the world.

Blessed are those called to the supper of the Lamb.

Priest and People (once only):

Lord, I am not worthy
that you should enter under my roof,
but only say the word
and my soul shall be healed.

Priest: The Body of Christ.

Communicant: **Amen.**

Priest: The Blood of Christ.

Communicant: **Amen.**

The Communion Chant or other appropriate song or hymn is sung while Communion is given to the faithful. If there is no singing, the Communion Antiphon is said.

STAND

Then, in the Prayer after Communion, the Priest prays in our name that we may live the life of faith since we have been strengthened by Christ himself. Our Amen makes his prayer our own.

Priest: Let us pray.

People: **Amen.**

THE CONCLUDING RITES

We have heard God's Word and eaten the Body of Christ. Now it is time for us to leave, to do good works, to praise and bless the Lord in our daily lives.

STAND

BLESSING AND DISMISSAL

Priest: The Lord be with you.

People: **And with your spirit.**

Priest: May almighty God bless you, the Father, and the Son, ✠ and the Holy Spirit.

People: **Amen.**

Deacon (or Priest):

(a) Go forth, the Mass is ended.

(b) Go and announce the Gospel of the Lord.

(c) Go in peace, glorifying the Lord by your life.

(d) Go in peace.

People: **Thanks be to God.**

COMMUNION PRAYERS

THE Eucharist is not only a Sacrifice but a spiritual banquet as well. Jesus renews His immolation in Holy Mass and gives us Himself as our spiritual nourishment (Jn 6:55, 54).

Communion is the most perfect participation in the Eucharistic Sacrifice and its most logical conclusion.

The divine effects which Communion produces in souls will be so much more complete and enduring the more fervent have been the preparation and thanksgiving for Communion.

Indeed, "union with Christ, to which the Sacrament itself is directed, is not to be limited to the duration of the celebra-

tion of the Eucharist; it is to be prolonged into the entire Christian life, in such a way that the Christian faithful, contemplating unceasingly the gift they have received, may make their life a continual thanksgiving under the guidance of the Holy Spirit and may produce fruits of greater charity" (*Instruction on the Eucharistic Mystery,* no. 38).

PRAYERS BEFORE HOLY COMMUNION

Act of Hope

GOOD Jesus, in You alone I place all my hope. You are my salvation and my strength, the Source of all good. Through Your mercy, through Your Passion and Death, I hope to obtain the pardon of my sins, the grace of final perseverance and a happy eternity.

Act of Love

JESUS, my God, I love You with my whole heart and

above all things, because you are the one supreme Good and an infinitely perfect Being. You have given your life for me, a poor sinner, and in Your mercy You have even offered Yourself as food for my soul.

My God, I love You. Inflame my heart to love You more.

Act of Contrition

O MY Savior, I am truly sorry for having offended You because You are infinitely good and sin displeases You. I detest all the sins of my life and I desire to atone for them. Through the merits of Your Precious Blood, wash from my soul all stain of sin, so that, cleansed in body and soul, I may worthily approach the Most Holy Sacrament of the Altar.

Act of Desire

JESUS, my God and my all, my soul longs for You. My heart yearns to receive You in Holy Communion. Come, Bread of heaven and Food of angels, to nourish my soul and to rejoice my heart. Come, most lovable Friend of my soul, to inflame me with such love that I may never again be separated from You.

Prayer of St. Thomas Aquinas

ALMIGHTY and eternal God, I approach the sacrament of Your only-begotten Son, our Lord Jesus Christ. As a sick man I approach the physician of life; as a man unclean, I come to the fountain of mercy; blind, to the light of eternal brightness; poor and needy, to the Lord of heaven and earth. I beseech You, therefore, in Your boundless mercy, to heal my sickness, to wash away my defilements, to enlighten my blindness, to enrich my poverty, and to clothe my nakedness.

Let me receive the Bread of angels, the King of kings, the Lord of lords, with such reverence and humility, such contrition and faith, such purpose and intention, as may help the salvation of my soul. Grant, I beseech You, that I may receive not only the Sacrament of the Body and Blood of our Lord, but also the whole grace and virtue of the Sacrament.

O most indulgent God, grant me so to receive the Body of Your only-begotten Son, our Lord, Jesus Christ, which He took of the

Virgin Mary, that I may be found worthy to be incorporated with His Mystical Body and numbered among His members.

O most loving Father, grant that I may one day forever contemplate Him unveiled and face to face, Whom, on my pilgrimage, I receive under a veil, Your beloved Son, Who lives and reigns with You and the Holy Spirit, one God, forever and ever.

PRAYERS AFTER HOLY COMMUNION

Act of Faith

JESUS, I firmly believe that You are present within me as God and Man, to enrich my soul with graces and to fill my heart with the happiness of the blessed. I believe that You are Christ, the Son of the living God!

Act of Adoration

WITH deepest humility, I adore You, my Lord and God; You have made my soul Your dwelling place. I adore You as my Creator from Whose hands I came and with Whom I long to be happy forever.

Act of Love

DEAR Jesus, I love You with my whole heart, my whole soul, and with all my strength. May the love of Your own Sacred Heart fill my soul and purify it so that I may die to the world for love of You, as You died on the Cross for love of me. My God, You are all mine; grant that I may be all Yours in time and in eternity.

Act of Thanksgiving

FROM the depths of my heart I thank You, dear Lord, for Your infinite kindness in coming to me. How good You are to me! With Your most holy Mother and all the angels, I praise Your mercy and generosity toward me, a poor sinner. I thank You for nourishing my soul with Your Sacred Body and Precious Blood. I will try to show my gratitude to You in the Sacrament of Your love, by obedience to Your holy commandments, by fidelity to my duties, by kindness to my neighbor and by an earnest endeavor to become like You in my daily conduct.

Prayer to Christ the King

O CHRIST Jesus, I acknowledge You as King of the

universe. All that has been created has been made for You. Exercise upon me all Your rights. I renew my baptismal promises, renouncing Satan and all his works and pomps. I promise to live a good Christian life and to be diligent in furthering the interests and teachings of Almighty God and Your Church.

Prayer of St. Thomas Aquinas

I THANK You, O holy Lord, almighty Father, eternal God, Who have deigned, not through any merit of mine, but out of the condescension of Your goodness, to nourish me a sinner, Your unworthy servant, with the Precious Body and Blood of Your Son, our Lord Jesus Christ.

I pray that this Holy Communion be not a condemnation to punishment for me, but a saving plea unto forgiveness.

May it be unto me the armor of faith and the shield of a good will. May it be the emptying out of my vices and the extinction of all lustful desires; an increase of charity and patience, of humility and obedience, and of all virtues; a strong defense against the snares of all my enemies, visible and invisible; the perfect quieting of all my evil impulses of flesh and spirit, binding me firmly to You, the one true God; and a happy ending of my life.

I pray too that You will deign to bring me a sinner to that ineffable banquet, where You, with Your Son and the Holy Spirit, are to Your Saints true light, fulfillment of desires, eternal joy, gladness without end, and perfect bliss. Through Christ our Lord.

Prayer to Our Redeemer

SOUL of Christ, sanctify me.
Body of Christ, save me.
Water from the side of Christ, wash me.
Blood of Christ, motivate me.
Passion of Christ, strengthen me.
O good Jesus, hear me.
Within Your wounds hide me.
Suffer me not to be separated from You.
From the malignant enemy, defend me.
At the hour of death, call me,
And bid me come to You,

That with Your saints I may praise
You
Forever and ever.

Prayer to Jesus Christ Crucified

BEHOLD, O kind and most sweet Jesus, I cast myself upon my knees in Your sight, and with the most fervent desire of my soul I pray and beseech You that You would impress upon my heart lively sentiments of Faith, Hope, and Charity, with true repentance for my sins, and a firm desire of amendment, while with deep affection and grief of soul I ponder within myself and mentally contemplate Your five most precious wounds, having before my eyes that which David spoke in prophecy of You, O good Jesus: They have pierced my hands and feet; they have numbered all my bones.

A *plenary indulgence* is granted on each Friday of Lent and Passiontide to the faithful, who after Communion piously recite the above prayer before an image of Christ crucified; on other days of the year the indulgence is *partial.*

Prayer to Jesus and Mary

O JESUS living in Mary, come and live in Your servants, in the spirit of Your holiness, in the fullness of Your power, in the perfection of Your ways, and in the truth of Your mysteries. Reign in us over all adverse power through Your Holy Spirit, and for the glory of the Father. Amen.

Mary, I come to you with child-like confidence and earnestly beg you to take me under your power-ful protection. Grant me a place in your loving motherly heart. I place my immortal soul into your hands and give you my own poor heart.

Prayer to St. Joseph

GUARDIAN of virgins, and holy father Joseph, to whose faithful custody Christ Jesus, innocence itself, and Mary, Virgin of virgins, were committed: I beg you, by these dear pledges, Jesus and Mary, that, being preserved from all uncleanness, I may with spotless mind, pure heart and chaste body ever serve Jesus and Mary most chastely all the days of my life. Amen.

VISITS TO JESUS IN THE BLESSED SACRAMENT

THROUGHOUT the course of the day we should strive to spend a few moments before Jesus in the Blessed Sacrament of the Altar. We should adore and thank Him for all the gifts that he has given us and for the gift of His Real Presence, then tell Him our needs and everything that is in our heart, so that we may receive comfort and strength.

The tabernacle is the Font of grace and mercy from which Jesus dispenses the benefit of His superabundant life and continually repeats to all: "Come to Me, all you who are weary and overburdened; and I will give you rest" (Mt 11:28).

The Eucharist is the sign of God's great love for us and fills us with happiness and gratitude. At the same time, it fills us with sorrow and pain because God's love is not returned by His people. The Heart which has so loved human beings remains neglected and even offended by them.

Conscious of this sad situation, we should make reparation for ourselves and for others. To make reparation signifies being united to Christ, taking up our cross and carrying it out of love for Him in atonement. Then our human love will dimly resemble divine love, becoming an eternal, universal, and saving love.

Act of Adoration

WE adore You, Most Holy Lord, Jesus Christ, here and in all the churches of the whole world, and we bless You because by Your holy Cross You have redeemed the world. Have mercy on us.

(St. Francis of Assisi)

Prayer of Adoration and Petition

I ADORE You, O Jesus, true God and true Man, here present in the Holy Eucharist, as I humbly kneel before You and unite myself in spirit with all the faithful on earth and all the Saints in heaven.

In heartfelt gratitude for so great a blessing, I love You, my Jesus, with my whole soul, for You are infinitely perfect and all worthy of my love. Give me the grace never more in any way to offend You. Grant that I may be renewed by Your Eucharistic presence here on earth and be found worthy to arrive with Mary at the enjoyment of Your eternal and blessed presence in heaven.

Prayer of Reparation

WITH that deep and humble feeling which the Faith inspires in me, O my God and Savior, Jesus Christ, true God and true Man, I love You with all my heart, and I adore You Who are hidden here. I do so in reparation for all the irreverences, profanations, and sacrileges which You receive in the most august Sacrament of the Altar.

I adore You, O my God, but not so much as You are worthy to be adored. Please accept my good will and help me in my weakness. Would that I could adore You with that perfect worship which the angels in heaven are able to offer You. O Jesus, may You be adored, loved, and thanked by all people at every moment in this most holy Sacrament.

Prayer for Today's Needs

LORD, for tomorrow and its needs I do not pray;
keep me, my God, from stain of sin, just for today.
Let me both diligently work and duly pray;
let me be kind in word and deed, just for today.
Let me be slow to do my will, prompt to obey;
help me to mortify my flesh, just for today.
Let me no wrong or idle word unthinking say;
set a seal upon my lips, just for today.
Let me in season, Lord, be grave, in season gay;

let me be faithful to Your grace,
just for today.
And if today my tide of life should
ebb away,
give me Your Sacraments divine,
sweet Lord, today.
So for tomorrow and its needs, I
do not pray;
but keep me, guide me, love me,
Lord, just for today.

Sister M. Xavier, S.N.D.

Prayer to Bring Christ into Our Day

LORD Jesus, present before me in the Sacrament of the Altar, help me to cast out from my mind all thoughts of which You do not approve and from my heart all emotions which You do not encourage. Enable me to spend my entire day as a co-worker with You, carrying out the tasks that You have entrusted to me.

Be with me at every moment of this day: during the long hours of work, that I may never tire or slacken from Your service; during my conversations, that they may not become for me occasions for meanness toward others; during the moments of worry and stress, that I may remain patient and spiritually calm; during periods of fatigue and illness, that I may avoid self-pity and think of others; during times of temptation, that I may take refuge in Your grace.

Help me to remain generous and loyal to You this day and so be able to offer it all up to You with its successes which I have achieved by Your help and its failures which have occurred through my own fault. Let me come to the wonderful realization that life is most real when it is lived with You as the Guest of my soul.

Invocations

PRAISE and adoration ever more be given to the most Holy Sacrament.

O SACRAMENT most holy, O Sacrament divine! All praise and all thanksgiving be every moment Thine!

RITE OF EUCHARISTIC EXPOSITION AND BENEDICTION

WHEN the faithful adore Christ present in the sacrament, they should remember that this presence derives from the sacrifice and is directed toward both sacramental and spiritual Communion.

In consequence, the devotion which leads the faithful to visit the Blessed Sacrament draws them into an ever deeper participation in the Paschal Mystery. It leads them to respond gratefully to the gift of Him Who through His humanity constantly pours divine life into the mem-

bers of His Body. Dwelling with Christ our Lord, they enjoy His intimate friendship and pour out their hearts before Him for themselves and their dear ones, and pray for the peace and salvation of the world.

They offer their entire lives with Christ to the Father in the Holy Spirit, and receive in this wonderful exchange an increase of faith, hope, and charity. Thus they nourish those right dispositions which enable them with all due devotion to celebrate the memorial of the Lord and receive frequently the heavenly Bread, Christ truly present, given us by the Father.

Down in Adoration Falling

DOWN in adoration falling,
Lo! the sacred Host we hail;
Lo! o'er ancient forms departing,
Newer rites of grace prevail;
Faith for all defects supplying,
Where the feeble senses fail.

To the everlasting Father,
And the Son Who reigns on high,
With the Holy Spirit proceeding
Forth from each eternally,
Be salvation, honor, blessing,
Might and endless majesty. Amen.

The minister then says a Prayer and concludes:

For ever and ever.
℟. **Amen.**

The Divine Praises

BLESSED be God.
Blessed be His holy Name.
Blessed be Jesus Christ, true God and true Man.
Blessed be the name of Jesus.
Blessed be His most Sacred Heart.
Blessed be His most Precious Blood.
Blessed be Jesus in the most holy Sacrament of the altar.

Blessed be the Holy Spirit, the Paraclete.

Blessed be the great Mother of God, Mary most holy.

Blessed be her holy and immaculate conception.

Blessed be her glorious assumption.

Blessed be the name of Mary, virgin and mother.

Blessed be St. Joseph, her most chaste spouse.

Blessed be God in His Angels and in His Saints.

THE RECEPTION OF HOLY COMMUNION OUTSIDE MASS

BELIEVING in Jesus Christ, we should desire to receive Him in Holy Communion, even when we cannot participate in the Mass. The sick and the aged especially should nourish themselves frequently on the Bread of Life.

Preparations for Communion

A suitable table covered with a cloth and provided with candles should be available when Communion is brought to a private home.

The Eucharist can be received under the appearance of wine by those who cannot receive the consecrated bread.

Eucharistic Fast

Communicants are not to receive the Sacrament unless they have fasted for one hour from solid food and beverages, with the exception of water.

The period of the eucharistic fast, that is, abstinence from food or alcoholic drink, is reduced to about a quarter of an hour for: (1) the sick who are living in hospitals or at home, even if they are not confined to bed; (2) the faithful of advanced age, even if not bedridden, whether they are confined to their homes because of old age or live in a nursing home; (3) sick priests, even if not bedridden, or elderly priests, whether they are to celebrate Mass or to receive Communion; (4) persons who care for the sick or aged, who wish to receive Communion with them, when they cannot conveniently observe the fast of one hour.

The Communion Service

The Communion Service begins with a short penitential rite, like that at Mass.

A celebration of the Word of God may then take place, comprising one or more readings, a psalm, a period of silence and some general intercessions.

After the Our Father is said together, the Sacrament is offered to the communicant. Presenting the Sacrament, the minister says "The Body of Christ." The communicant answers "Amen."

A short prayer and concluding rite follow.

Meditation on the Eucharist

WHILE they were eating He took bread, and after He had pronounced the blessing, He broke it and gave it to them, saying "Take it; this is My Body." Then He took a cup, and after offering thanks He gave it to them. After they all drank from it, He said to them, "This is My Blood of the Covenant, which will be shed on behalf of many. Amen, I say to you, from now on I shall not drink this fruit of the vine until the day when I shall drink it anew in the Kingdom of God" (Mark 14:22-25).

Meaning of the Eucharist

SINCE it was the will of God's only-begotten Son that human beings should share in His Divinity, He assumed our nature in order that by becoming Human He might make humans gods. Moreover, when He took our flesh He dedicated the whole of its substance to our salvation.

He offered His Body to God the Father on the altar of the cross as a sacrifice for our reconciliation. He shed His Blood for our ransom and purification, so that we might be redeemed from our wretched state of bondage and cleansed from all sin.

But to ensure that the memory of so great a gift would abide with us forever, He left His Body as food and His Blood as drink for the faithful to consume in the form of bread and wine.

O precious and wonderful banquet, that brings us salvation and contains all sweetness! Could anything be of more intrinsic value? Under the old law it was the flesh of calves and goats that was offered, but here Christ Himself, the true God, is set before us as our food. What could be more wonderful than this?

No other Sacrament has greater healing power; through it sins are purged away, virtues are increased, and the soul is enriched with an abundance of every spiritual gift. It is offered in the Church for the living and the dead, so that what was instituted for the salvation of all may benefit all.

Yet, in the end, no one can fully express the sweetness of this Sacrament, in which spiritual delight is tasted at its source, and in which we renew the memory of that surpassing love for us which Christ revealed in His Passion.

It was to impress the vastness of this love more firmly upon the hearts of the faithful that our Lord instituted this Sacrament at the Last Supper. As He was on the point of leaving the world to go to the Father, after celebrating the Passover with His disciples, He left it as a perpetual Memorial of His Passion.

It was the fulfillment of ancient figures and the greatest of all His miracles, while for those who were to experience the sorrow of His departure, it was destined to be a unique and abiding consolation.

St. Thomas Aquinas

Prayer of Thanksgiving and Petition

WE give you thanks, O Christ, our God; in Your goodness You have given us Your Body in this Sacrament to enable us to live holy lives. Through Your grace keep us pure and without stain. Remain in us to protect us. Direct our steps in the way of Your holy and benevolent will.

CONFESSION PRAYERS

CHRISTIAN penance is above all an interior virtue, an attitude of struggle against sin, a willingness to be converted when we have drawn away from God, and a constant desire to realize in ourselves the requirements of Baptism in order to participate in the mystery of Christ's Death so that we may live the new life in the Spirit.

The Sacrament of Penance requires a real response from us—a desire to change. This is aided by hearing the Word of God. Through this Word, Christians receive light to recognize their sins and are called to conversion and to confidence in God's loving mercy.

The Sermon on the Mount — "When Jesus saw the crowds, He went up on the mountain. After He was seated, His disciples gathered around him. Then He began to teach them." — *Mt 5:1f.*

Jesus Blesses the Children — " 'Let the little children come to Me; do not hinder them. For it is to such as these that the Kingdom of God belongs'. . . . And [He] blessed them" — *Mk 10:14ff.*

Jesus Our Consoler — "Come to Me, all you who are weary and overburdened, and I will give you rest. . . . You will find rest for your souls" — *Mt 11:28f.*

The Cleansing of the Temple — Jesus "began to drive out those who were engaging in selling saying: . . . 'My house shall be a house of prayer' but you have made it a 'den of thieves" — *Lk 19:45f.*

Thus, this Sacrament now contains a more communitarian dimension, showing that it is part of the Church's work of reconciling sinners to God. It also contains elements of thanksgiving and praise to God for salvation. Finally, it shines out with the paschal joy of those who have been redeemed by the Son of God.

When we go to confession, we should:

1) Ask ourselves how we have offended God.

2) Be truly sorry for our sins.

3) Make up our minds not to sin again.

4) Tell our sins to the priest.

5) Do the penance the priest gives us.

PRAYER BEFORE CONFESSION

MY Lord and God, I have sinned. I am guilty before You.

Grant me the strength to say to Your minister what I say to You in the secret of my heart.

Increase my repentance. Make it more genuine. May it be really a sorrow for having offended You and my neighbor rather than a wounded love of self.

Help me to atone for my sin. May the sufferings of my life and my little mortifications be joined with the sufferings of Jesus, Your Son, and cooperate in rooting sin from the world.

EXAMINATION OF CONSCIENCE

How long has it been since my last confession?

Did I conceal any sin?

Did I say my penance?

Have I neglected my home and my family duties, or my work?

Have I been lazy, neglectful, or willfully distracted during prayer or at Mass?

Have I used God's name irreverently, or taken false or needless oaths?

Have I missed Mass through my own fault on Sundays or holydays, or worked unnecessarily on Sunday?

Have I disobeyed, angered, or been disrespectful toward my parents, teachers, employers, or other superiors?

Have I been unjust and unkind to those over whom I have authority?

Have I quarreled with or willfully hurt anyone?

Have I been guilty of cruelty, mental or physical, toward anyone?

Have I caused another to commit sin?

Have I offended in any way by thought, word, or deed against purity?

Have I led others into sin?

Have I stolen or destroyed property belonging to any other person or company?

Have I given a bad example to the members of my family or others?

Have I knowingly accepted stolen goods?

Have I paid all my just debts?

Have I told lies, repeated harmful gossip, or injured another person's character?

Have I been sinfully angry, greedy, proud, envious, jealous, or intemperate in eating or drinking?

Have I willfully broken any of the Church laws concerning fast or abstinence?

Have I failed to support my Church?

Have I received Communion during Easter Time?

For married people:

Have I failed to show love, respect, and good example toward my partner?

Have I neglected my duty to my children in regard to their religious instruction, to their training in good habits, and to their schooling?

Have I sinned against the duties of married life?

We must confess **the number of our sins as best we can remember them.**

CELEBRATION OF THE SACRAMENT OF PENANCE

1. Reception of the Penitent

Penitent:

In the name of the Father, and of the Son, and of the Holy Spirit. Amen.

Priest:

May the grace of the Holy Spirit
fill your heart with light,
that you may confess your sins with loving trust
and come to know that God is merciful.

Penitent: **Amen.**

2. Reading of the Word of God

Priest:

After John's arrest, Jesus appeared in Galilee proclaiming the good news of God: "This is the time of fulfillment. The reign of God is at hand! Reform your lives and believe in the gospel!" (Mark 1:14-15).

(Another reading may be used.)

3. Confession of Sins

The penitent confesses his sins; the priest accepts the confession and imposes a penance. The penitent then expresses sorrow for sins in these or similar words:

Penitent:

I am sorry for my sins with all my heart.
In choosing to do wrong
and failing to do good,
I have sinned against you
whom I should love above all things.
I firmly intend, with your help,

to do penance,
to sin no more,
and to avoid whatever leads me to sin.
Our Savior Jesus Christ
suffered and died for us.
In his name, my God, have mercy.

4. Absolution

Priest:

GOD, the Father of mercies,
through the death and resurrection
of his Son.
has reconciled the world to himself
and sent the Holy Spirit among us
for the forgiveness of sins;
through the ministry of the Church
may God give you pardon and peace,
and I absolve you from your sins
in the name of the Father, and of the Son,
and of the Holy Spirit. Amen.

5. Proclamation of Praise of God and Dismissal

Priest:
Give thanks to the Lord for he is good.

Penitent:
His mercy endures for ever.

Thanksgiving after Confession

MY dearest Jesus, I have told all my sins as well as I could. I have tried hard to make a good confession. I feel sure that You have forgiven me. I thank You. It is only because of all Your sufferings that I can go to confession and free myself from my sins. Your Heart is full of love and mercy for poor sinners. I love You because You are so good to me.

My loving Savior, I shall try to keep from sin and to love You more each day.

My dear Mother Mary, pray for me and help me to keep my promises. Protect me and do not let me fall back into sin.

DEVOTIONAL PRAYERS

PRAYERS TO THE BLESSED TRINITY

OUR prayer life should manifest the fact that the Blessed Trinity constitutes the central reality for Christians. Our entire lives are lived in the loving embrace of Father, Son, and Holy Spirit.

God the Father is the Creator, God the Son is the Redeemer, and God the Holy Spirit is the Sanctifier—but not in such a way that the Son and the Holy Spirit are excluded from creation, or the Father and the Holy Spirit from redemption, or the Father and the Son from sanctification.

Prayer in Praise of the Trinity

I VENERATE and glorify You, O most Blessed Trinity, in union with that ineffable glory with which God the Father, in His omnipotence, honors the Holy Spirit forever.

I magnify and bless You, O most Blessed Trinity, in union with that most reverent glory with which God the Son, in His ineffable wisdom, glorifies the Father and the Holy Spirit forever.

I adore and extol You, O most Blessed Trinity, in union with that most adequate and befitting glory with which the Holy Spirit, in His unchangeable goodness, extols the Father and the Son forever.

Prayer to Be Conformed to the Divine Will

MOST holy Trinity, Godhead indivisible, Father, Son, and Holy Spirit, our first beginning and our last end, You have made us in accord with your own image and likeness.

Grant that all the thoughts of our minds, all the words of our tongues, all the affections of our hearts, and all the actions of our being may always be conformed to Your holy will.

Thus, after we have seen You here below in creation and in a dark manner by means of faith, we may come at last to contemplate You face-to-face forever in heaven.

Prayer of Consecration to the Trinity

O GOD, I vow and consecrate to You all that is in me: my memory and my actions to God the Father; my understanding and my words to God the Son; my will and my thoughts to God the Holy Spirit; my heart and my body, my tongue, my senses, and all my sorrows to the sacred humanity of Jesus Christ, Who was content to be betrayed into the hands of wicked men and to suffer the torment of the Cross.

St. Francis de Sales

PRAYERS TO GOD THE FATHER

By nature God is our Creator and Lord, and we are His creatures and subjects. As a result of sin, however, we have become His enemies and deserve His chastisements. Yet, through the grace of

Christ, the Father lovingly pardons us, adopts us as His children, and destines us to share in the life and beatitude of that same Christ, His only-begotten Son.

Prayer to the Father enables us to balance His supreme perfections and transcendence with His loving concern for the least of His creatures.

Prayer of Praise and Petition

WE praise You, invisible Father, giver of immortality, and source of life and light. You love all human beings, especially the poor. You seek reconciliation with all of them and You draw them to yourself by sending Your beloved Son to visit them.

Make us really alive by giving us the light to know You, the only true God, and Jesus Christ Whom You have sent. Grant us the Holy

Spirit and enable us to speak volumes about Your ineffable mysteries.

St. Serapion of Thmuis

Prayer to the Father for the Benefits of Christ's Redemption

ETERNAL Father, I offer You the infinite satisfaction which Jesus rendered to your justice in behalf of sinners on the tree of the Cross. I ask that You would make available the merits of His Precious Blood to all guilty souls to whom sin has brought death. May they rise again to the life of grace and glorify You forever.

Prayer of Thanks for the Father's Love

ETERNAL Father, we thank You for Your great love. You give the world the best of Yourself, the mirror of Your perfect transparency, the splendor of Your very being—Your Son Jesus.

We thank You for giving Jesus to us as our Savior, not as a tyrant but as a friend, not as a superior but as a brother.

Help us to open our hearts to His light without fear of being overwhelmed but exultant with the joy that comes from this light upon all who accept it with gladness.

Prayer to the Father for Reconciliation

HEAVENLY Father, in the death and resurrection of Jesus Christ Your Son You willed to reconcile all mankind to Yourself and so to reconcile all human beings with each other in peace. Hear the prayer of Your people.

Let Your spirit of life and holiness renew us in the depths of our being and unite us throughout our life to the risen Christ: for He is our Brother and Savior.

With all Christians we seek to follow the way of the Gospel. Keep us faithful to the teachings of the Church and alive to the needs of our neighbors. Give us strength to work for reconciliation, unity, and peace.

May those who seek the God they do not yet know discover in You the source of light and hope. May those who work for others find strength in You. May those who already know You seek even further and experience the depths of Your love.

Forgive us our sins, deepen our faith, kindle our hope, and enliven our hearts with love. May we walk in the footsteps of Jesus as Your beloved sons and daughters.

With the help of Mary, our Mother, may Your Church be the sign and sacrament of salvation for all people, that the world may believe in Your love and Your truth.

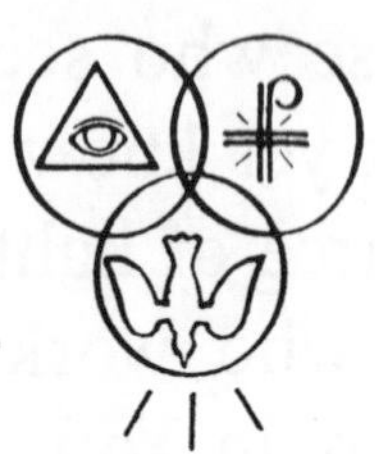

PRAYERS TO GOD THE SON

Our knowledge of God is communicated to us by God the Son made Man, Jesus Christ. In Him we have access to the Father. By entrusting ourselves to Him in prayer we attain our true goal in life.

Jesus poured out on His people the Spirit of adoption by making us children of God. United with Jesus, this new people of God constitutes "the whole Christ." He offers them to His Father and gives Him glory. This is the aim of His Father's plan for the salvation of all.

Prayer to Jesus, True Man

O JESUS, You are true Man. You took upon Yourself a human body and soul, You thought with a human mind, and You acted through a human will.

But You are far above every other human. No one ever spoke like You, with such authority, freedom, and gentleness, indicating the paths of love, justice, and sincerity. And no one ever matched Your teachings.

You spoke about the mystery of God in a way so elevated above others that You make it possible for us to come to know God and achieve a living love for Him.

O Jesus, no one ever acted like You, either. You left us an example of the perfect human life: by Your preference for poverty, by Your love for the poor and the sick, by Your concern for the suffering, by Your liberating message of salvation, by Your espousal of peace and service, by Your obedience to the Father—even to the death of the Cross.

O Jesus, help us to know You more. Help us to live with You so that we may live fully human lives. Satisfy us with Yourself, the Man for others, and with God, perfect Love—the Man-Who-is-Love, and God-Who-is-Love.

Prayer to Jesus, True God

O JESUS, You are the Son of God. You resolve our problems and respond to our aspirations with unexpected fullness.

As the Son sent to us by the Father, You are the God Who comes to meet us and manifests for us the God Whom we seek.

You are the revelation of God for us—the full, perfect, and definitive revelation—God in person.

In You the God-Who-is-far-off becomes the God-Who-is-near, the God-with-us, and the God-Who-is-one-of-us, our companion of life's journey. You alone, O Lord, are the Way, the Truth, and the Life, the Messiah, and the Son of the living God.

Petitions to Jesus

O GOOD Jesus:
Word of the eternal Father, convert me.
Son of Mary, take me as her child.
My Master, teach me.
Prince of peace, give me peace.
My Refuge, receive me.

My Shepherd, feed my soul.
Model of patience, comfort me.
Meek and humble of heart, help me to become like You.
My Redeemer, save me.
My God and my All, possess me.
The true Way, direct me.
Eternal Truth, instruct me.
Life of the saints, make me live in You.
My Support, strengthen me.
My Justice, justify me.
My Mediator with the Father, reconcile me.
Physician of my soul, heal me.
My Judge, pardon me.
My King, rule me.
My Sanctification, sanctify me.
Abyss of goodness, pardon me.
Living Bread of heaven, feed me.
Father of the prodigal, receive me.

Joy of my soul, be my only happiness.
My Helper, assist me.
Magnet of love, draw me.
My Protector, defend me.
My Hope, sustain me.
Object of my love, unite me to Yourself.
Fountain of life, refresh me.
My Divine Victim, atone for me.
My Last End, let me possess You.
My Glory, glorify me.

Prayer to the Miraculous Infant of Prague

DEAR Jesus, Little Infant of Prague, how tenderly You love us! Your greatest joy is to dwell among us and to bestow Your blessing upon us. So many who turned to You with confidence have received graces and had their petitions granted. I also come before You now with this special request (*mention it*).

Dear Infant, rule over me and do with me and mine as You will, for I know that in Your divine wisdom and love You will arrange everything for the best. Do not withdraw Your hand from me, but protect me and bless me forever.

Dear Infant, help me in my needs. Make me truly happy with You in time and in eternity, and I shall thank You forever with all my heart.

Prayer of Praise to the Holy Name of Jesus

O GLORIOUS Name of Jesus, gracious Name, Name of love and of power! Through You sins are forgiven, enemies are vanquished, the sick are freed from illness, the suffering are made strong and cheerful. You bring honor to those who believe, instruction to those who preach, strength to those who toil, and sustenance to those who are weary.

Our love for You is ardent and glowing, our prayers are heard, the souls of those who contemplate You are filled to overflowing, and all the blessed in heaven are filled with Your glory. Grant that we too may reign with them through this Your most holy Name.

Prayer to the Crucified Christ

LORD Jesus hanging on the Cross, I raise sorrowful and shameful eyes to You. You have granted me untold blessings and I have repaid You by contributing to Your Passion and death. My hands took part in Your scourging, my voice was among those who denied You and called for Your death, my thoughts, brought about Your crowning with thorns, my sins drove the nails into Your hands and feet, and the lance into Your side.

Dear Lord, forgive me for all these sins. You are great, glorious, and infinitely good; I am insignificant, selfish, and hopelessly sinful. But I am sorry for all my sins, and by the Blood shed in Your Passion I beg for forgiveness and for a share in Your love and grace.

Prayer of the Seven Last Words

O DIVINE Jesus, incarnate Son of God, for our salvation You consented to be born in a stable, to spend Your whole life amid poverty, trials, and misery, and to die surrounded by sufferings on the Cross. At the hour of my death, please say to Your Father: *Father, forgive him/her.* Say to Your beloved Mother: *Behold your son/daughter.* Say to my soul: *This day you shall be with Me in paradise.*

My God, my God, do not forsake me in that hour. *I thirst,* yes, my soul thirsts for You Who are the fountain of living waters. My life passes away like a shadow; in a short while *everything will be accomplished.* Therefore my adorable Savior, from this moment and for all eternity *into Your hands I commend my spirit.* Lord Jesus, receive my soul.

Prayer in Honor of the Precious Blood

PRECIOUS Blood of Jesus, infinite price of our redemption and both the drink and the laver of our souls, You continually plead the cause of all people before the throne of infinite mercy. From the depths of my heart I adore You. Jesus, insofar as I am able I want to make reparation for the insults and outrages which You receive from human beings, especially from those who blaspheme You.

Who would not venerate this Blood of infinite value! Who does not feel inflamed with love for Jesus Who shed it! What would have become of me had I not been redeemed by this divine Blood! Who has drained it all from the veins of my Savior? Surely this was the work of love!

O infinite love, which has given us this saving balm! O balm beyond all price, welling up from the fountain of infinite love! Grant that every heart and every tongue may render You praise and thanks now and forever!

PRAYERS TO THE SACRED HEART OF JESUS

THE Heart of Jesus is the symbol of the infinite love that impelled the Son of God to become our brother, to die for us on the Cross, and to remain forever in the Sacrament of the Altar. Jesus asks each of us to return that love.

The Promises of the Sacred Heart

In various appearances to St. Margaret Mary Alacoque, Jesus manifested His great love for human beings and made the following promises to those who give particular honor to His Sacred Heart.

1. I will give them all the graces necessary in their state of life.

2. I will establish peace in their homes.

3. I will comfort them in all their afflictions.

4. I will be their secure refuge during life, and above all in death.

5. I will bestow abundant blessings upon all their undertakings.

6. Sinners shall find in My Heart the source and the infinite ocean of mercy.

7. Tepid souls shall become fervent.

8. Fervent souls shall quickly mount to high perfection.

9. I will bless every place in which an image of My Heart shall be exposed and honored.

10. I will give to priests the gift of touching the most hardened hearts.

11. Those who shall promote this devotion shall have their names written in My Heart, never to be effaced.

12. I promise you in the excessive mercy of My Heart that My all-powerful love will grant to all those who communicate on the First Friday in nine consecutive months the grace of final penitence; they shall not die

in My disgrace nor without receiving their Sacraments. My divine Heart shall be their safe refuge in this last moment.

Prayer to the Sacred Heart for Perseverance

O SACRED Heart of Jesus, living and life-giving fountain of eternal life, infinite treasure of the Divinity, and glowing furnace of love, You are my refuge and my sanctuary. O adorable and glorious Savior, consume my heart with that burning fire that ever inflames Your Heart.

Pour down on my soul those graces which flow from Your love. Let my heart be so united with Yours that our wills may be one, and mine may in all things be conformed to Yours. May Your Will be the rule of both my desires and my actions. *St. Alphonsus Liguori*

Prayer of Trust in the Sacred Heart

IN all my temptations, I place my trust in You, O Sacred Heart of Jesus.

In all my weaknesses, I place my trust in You, O Sacred Heart of Jesus.

In all my difficulties, I place my trust in You, O Sacred Heart of Jesus.

In all my trials, I place my trust in You, O Sacred Heart of Jesus.

In all my sorrows, I place my trust in You, O Sacred Heart of Jesus.

In all my work, I place my trust in You, O Sacred Heart of Jesus.

In every failure, I place my trust in You, O Sacred Heart of Jesus.

In every discouragement, I place my trust in You, O Sacred Heart of Jesus.

In life and in death, I place my trust in You, O Sacred Heart of Jesus.

In time and in eternity, I place my trust in You, O Sacred Heart of Jesus.

Act of Dedication of the Human Race to Christ the King

MOST sweet Jesus, Redeemer of the human race, look down upon us humbly prostrate before You. We are Yours, and Yours we wish to be; but to be more surely united with You, behold, each one of us freely consecrates himself today to Your Most Sacred Heart.

Many indeed have never known You; many, too, despising Your precepts, have rejected You. Have mercy on them all, most merciful Jesus, and draw them to Your Sacred Heart.

Be King, O Lord, not only of the faithful who have never forsaken You, but also of the prodigal children who have abandoned You; grant that they may quickly return to their Father's house, lest they die of wretchedness and hunger.

Be King of those who are deceived by erroneous opinions, or whom discord keeps aloof, and call them back to the harbor of truth and the unity of faith, so that soon there may be but one flock and one Shepherd.

Grant, O Lord, to Your Church assurance of freedom and immunity from harm; give tranquility of order to all nations; make the earth resound from pole to pole with one cry: Praise to the divine Heart that wrought our salvation; to it be glory and honor forever. Amen.

A* partial indulgence *is granted to the faithful, who piously recite the above Act of Dedication of the Human Race to Christ the King. A* plenary indulgence *is granted, if it is recited publicly on the feast of Christ the King.

Litany of the Most Sacred Heart of Jesus

LORD, have mercy.
Christ, have mercy.
Lord, have mercy.
Christ, hear us.
Christ, graciously hear us.

God, the Father of heaven,
*have mercy on us.**

God the Son, Redeemer of the world,

God, the Holy Spirit,

Holy Trinity, one God,

Heart of Jesus, Son of the eternal Father,

Heart of Jesus, formed by the Holy Spirit in the womb of the Virgin Mother,

Heart of Jesus, substantially united to the Word of God,

Heart of Jesus, of infinite majesty,

Heart of Jesus, sacred temple of God,

Heart of Jesus, tabernacle of the Most High,

Heart of Jesus, house of God and gate of heaven,

* *"Have mercy on us" is repeated after each invocation.*

Heart of Jesus, burning furnace of love,
Heart of Jesus, abode of justice and love,
Heart of Jesus, full of goodness and love,
Heart of Jesus, abyss of all virtues,
Heart of Jesus, most worthy of all praise,
Heart of Jesus, King and center of all hearts,
Heart of Jesus, in Whom are all the treasures of wisdom and knowledge,
Heart of Jesus, in Whom dwells the fullness of Divinity,
Heart of Jesus, in Whom the Father was well pleased,
Heart of Jesus, of Whose fullness we have all received,

Heart of Jesus, desire of the everlasting hills,
Heart of Jesus, patient and most merciful,
Heart of Jesus, enriching all who invoke You,
Heart of Jesus, fountain of life and holiness,
Heart of Jesus, propitiation for our sins,
Heart of Jesus, loaded down with opprobrium,
Heart of Jesus, bruised for our offenses,
Heart of Jesus, obedient to death,
Heart of Jesus, pierced with a lance,
Heart of Jesus, source of all consolation,
Heart of Jesus, our life and resurrection,

Heart of Jesus, our peace and reconciliation,

Heart of Jesus, victim for our sins,

Heart of Jesus, salvation of those who trust in You,

Heart of Jesus, hope of those who die in You,

Heart of Jesus, delight of all the Saints,

Lamb of God, You take away the sins of the world; *spare us, O Lord.*

Lamb of God, You take away the sins of the world; *graciously hear us, O Lord.*

Lamb of God, You take away the sins of the world; *have mercy on us.*

℣. Jesus, meek and humble of heart.

℟. *Make our hearts like to Yours.*

LET us pray. Almighty and eternal God, look upon the Heart of Your most beloved Son and upon the praises and satisfaction which He offers You in the name of sinners; and to those who implore Your mercy, in Your great goodness, grant forgiveness in the name of the same Jesus Christ, Your Son, Who lives and reigns with You forever and ever.

THE STATIONS OF THE CROSS

THE Stations of the Cross is a devotion to the Sacred Passion, in which we accompany, in spirit, our Blessed Lord in His sorrowful journey from the house of Pilate to Calvary, and meditate on His sufferings and death.

Before each Station genuflect and say: "We adore You, O Christ, and we bless You; because by Your holy Cross, You have redeemed the world." Then meditate upon the scene before you for a few moments. The short prayers for each Station may be helpful.

1. Jesus Is Condemned to Death

O Jesus, You desired to die for me that I may receive supernatural life, sanctifying grace, and become a child of God. How precious must be that life. Teach me to appreciate it more and help me never to lose it by sin.

2. Jesus Bears His Cross

O Jesus, You have chosen to die the disgraceful death on the Cross. You have paid a high price for my redemption and the life of grace that was bestowed upon me. May I love You always and bear my crosses for Your sake.

3. Jesus Falls the First Time

O Jesus, Your painful fall under the Cross and Your quick rise teach me to repent and rise instantly should I ever be forgetful of Your love and commit a mortal sin. Make me strong enough to conquer my wicked passions.

4. Jesus Meets His Mother

O Jesus, Your afflicted Mother was resigned to Your Passion because she is my Mother also, and wants to see me live and die as a child of God. Grant me a tender love for You and Your holy Mother.

5. Jesus Is Helped by Simon

O Jesus, Simon first reluctantly helped You to carry the Cross. Make me better understand the value of my sufferings which should lead me closer to You, as Simon was united with You through the Cross.

6. Jesus and Veronica

O Jesus, how graciously did You reward that courageous woman. When I side with You against sin and temptation, You surely will increase the beauty of my soul and fill me with joy and peace. Jesus, give me courage.

7. Jesus Falls a Second Time

O Jesus, despite my good resolutions I have sinned repeatedly. But Your sufferings assure me of forgiveness if only I return to You with a contrite heart. I repent for having offended You. Help me to avoid sin in the future.

8. Jesus Speaks to the Women

O Jesus, You told the women of Jerusalem to weep for their sins rather than for You. Make me weep for my sins which caused Your terrible sufferings and the loss of my friendship with You.

9. Jesus Falls a Third Time

O Jesus, I see You bowed to the earth, enduring the pains of extreme exhaustion. Grant that I may never yield to despair in time of hardship and spiritual distress. Let me come to You for help and comfort.

10. Jesus Is Stripped of His Garments

O Jesus, You permitted Yourself to be stripped of Your garments. Strip me of sin and clothe me with Your holiness. Grant that I may sacrifice all my unlawful attachments rather than imperil the divine life of my soul.

11. Jesus Is Nailed to the Cross

O Jesus, how could I complain if nailed to God's commandments which are given for my salvation, when I see You nailed to the Cross! Strengthen my faith and increase my love for You. Help me keep the commandments.

12. Jesus Dies on the Cross

O Jesus, dying on the Cross, You preached love and forgiveness. May I be thankful that You have made me a child of God. Help me to forgive all who have injured me, so that I myself may obtain forgiveness.

13. Jesus Is Taken from the Cross

O Jesus, a sword of grief pierced Your Mother's heart when You were lying lifeless in her arms. Grant me through her intercession to lead the life of a loyal child of Mary, so that I may be received by her at my death.

14. Jesus Is Placed in the Sepulcher

O Jesus, Your enemies triumphed when they sealed Your tomb. But Your eternal triumph began on Easter morning. Strengthen my good will to live for You until the divine life of my soul will be manifested in heaven.

"All were filled with the Holy Spirit."

PRAYERS TO THE HOLY SPIRIT

BEFORE ascending to the Father, Jesus told His Apostles that He would send them the Holy Spirit Who would be with them forever.

On the day of Pentecost, the Spirit of love and truth descended upon the Apostles gathered in the Upper Room and filled them with power and light.

The Holy Spirit comes to each disciple of Christ and takes possession of every soul that opens to His grace. We must strive to be open and docile to the sanctifying action of God's Spirit in us.

Prayer to Receive the Holy Spirit

O KING of glory, send us the Promised of the Father, the Spirit of Truth. May the Counselor Who proceeds from You enlighten us and infuse all truth in us, as You have promised.

For the Seven Gifts of the Spirit

O LORD Jesus, through You I humbly beg our merciful Father to send the Holy Spirit of grace, that He may bestow upon us His sevenfold gifts.

May He send us the gift of *wisdom* which will make us relish the Tree of Life that is none other than Yourself; the gift of *understanding* which will enlighten us; the gift of *counsel* which will guide us in the way of righteousness; and the gift of *fortitude* which will give us the strength to vanquish the enemies of our sanctification and salvation.

May He impart to us the gift of *knowledge* which will enable us to discern Your teaching and distinguish good from evil; the gift of *piety* which will make us enjoy true peace; and the *gift of fear* which will make us shun all iniquity and avoid all danger of offending Your Majesty.

To the Father and to the Son and to the Holy Spirit be given all glory and thanksgiving forever.

St. Bonaventure

For the Twelve Fruits of the Spirit

HOLY Spirit, eternal Love of the Father and the Son,

kindly bestow on us the fruit of *charity,* that we may be united to You by divine love; the fruit of *joy,* that we may be filled with holy consolation; the fruit of *peace,* that we may enjoy tranquility of soul; and the fruit of *patience,* that we may endure humbly everything that may be opposed to our own desires.

Divine Spirit, be pleased to infuse in us the fruit of *benignity,* that we may willingly relieve our neighbor's necessities; the fruit of *goodness,* that we may be benevolent toward all; the fruit of *longanimity,* that we may not be discouraged by delay but may persevere in prayer; and the fruit of *mildness,* that we may subdue every rising of ill temper, stifle every murmur, and repress the susceptibilities of our nature in all our dealings with our neighbor.

Creator Spirit, graciously impart to us the fruit of *fidelity,* that we may rely with assured confidence on the word of God; the fruit of *modesty,* that we may act becomingly; and the fruits of *continence* and *chastity,* that we may keep our bodies in such holiness as befits Your temple, so that, having by Your assistance preserved our hearts pure on earth, we may merit in Jesus Christ, according to the words of the Gospel, to see God eternally in the glory of His Kingdom.

Prayer for Union with the Holy Spirit

O HOLY Spirit of Light and Love, to You I consecrate my heart, mind, and will for time and eternity. May I be ever docile to Your divine inspirations and to the teachings of the holy Catholic Church whose infallible guide You are.

May my heart be ever inflamed with the love of God and love of neighbor. May my will be ever in harmony with Your divine Will. May my life faithfully imitate the life and virtues of our Lord and Savior Jesus Christ. To Him, with the Father, and You, divine Spirit, be honor and glory forever.

St. Pius X

Archconfraternity Prayer to the Holy Spirit

HOLY Spirit, Lord of Light,
from Your clear celestial height,
Your pure beaming radiance give.
Come, O Father of the Poor,
come with treasures which endure,
come, O Light of all that live.
You of all Consolers best,
and the soul's delightsome Guest,
do refreshing Peace bestow.
You in toil are Comfort sweet,
pleasant Coolness in the heat,
solace in the midst of woe.
Light immortal, Light Divine,
visit now this heart of mine,
and my inmost being fill.
If You take Your grace away,
nothing pure in men will stay,

all their good is turned to ill.
Heal our wounds, our strength renew,
on our dryness pour Your dew,
wash the stains of guilt away.
Bend the stubborn heart and will,
melt the frozen, warm the chill,
guide the steps that go astray.
On all those who evermore
You confess and You adore,
in Your *Sevenfold Gifts* descend.
Give them Comfort when they die.
Give them Life with You on high,
give them Joys which never end.

Prayer for the Indwelling of the Spirit

HOLY Spirit, powerful Consoler, sacred Bond of the Father and the Son, Hope of the afflicted, descend into my heart and establish in it Your loving dominion. Enkindle in my tepid soul the fire of Your Love so that I may be wholly subject to You.

We believe that when You dwell in us, You also prepare a dwelling for the Father and the Son. Deign, therefore, to come to me, Consoler of abandoned souls and Protector of the needy. Help the afflicted, strengthen the weak, and support the wavering.

Come and purify me. Let no evil desire take possession of me. You love the humble and resist the proud. Come to me, glory of the living and hope of the dying. Lead me by Your grace that I may always be pleasing to You.

St. Augustine of Hippo

Mother of our Savior, pray for us.

PRAYERS TO THE BLESSED VIRGIN MARY

"Devotion to the Blessed Virgin is firmly rooted in the revealed Word and has solid dogmatic foundations. It is based on the singular dignity of Mary, Mother of the Son of God, and therefore beloved daughter of the Father and Temple of the Holy Spirit—Mary who, because of this extraordinary grace, is far greater than any other creature on earth or in heaven" (*Paul VI: Devotion to the Blessed Virgin Mary,* no. 56).

"When Mary is honored, her Son is duly acknowledged, loved and glorified, and His commandments are observed. To venerate Mary correctly means to acknowledge her Son, for she is the Mother

of God. To love her means to love Jesus, for she is always the Mother of Jesus.

"To pray to our Lady means not to substitute her for Christ, but to glorify her Son who desires us to have loving confidence in His Saints, especially in His Mother. To imitate the 'faithful Virgin' means to keep her Son's commandments." ***(U.S. Bishops: Behold Your Mother, No. 82)***

Hail, Holy Queen *(See p. 20)*

We Fly to Your Patronage

WE fly to your patronage, O holy Mother of God; despise not our petitions in our necessities, but deliver us always from all dangers, O glorious and blessed Virgin.

Mary, Mother of Grace

MARY, Mother of grace, Mother of mercy, shield me from the enemy and receive me at the hour of my death.

Holy Mary, Help the Helpless

HOLY Mary, help the helpless, strengthen the fearful, comfort the sorrowful, pray for the people, plead for the clergy, intercede for all women consecrated to God; may all who keep your sacred commemoration experience the might of your assistance.

Partial indulgence.

Remember, O Most Gracious Virgin Mary (The "Memorare")

REMEMBER, O most gracious Virgin Mary, that never was it known that anyone who fled to your protection, implored your help or sought your intercession was left unaided. Inspired with this confidence, I fly to you, O Virgin of virgins, my Mother; to you do I come, before you I stand, sinful and sorrowful. O Mother of the Word Incarnate, despise not my petitions, but in your mercy hear and answer me. Amen.

Partial indulgence.

Prayer to Our Lady of Fatima

O MOST holy Virgin Mary, Queen of the most holy Rosary, you were pleased to appear to the children of Fatima and reveal a glorious message. We implore you, inspire in our hearts a fervent love for the recitation of the Rosary. By meditating on the mysteries of the redemption that are recalled therein may we obtain the graces and virtues that we ask, through the merits of Jesus Christ, our Lord and Redeemer.

Prayer to Our Lady of Good Counsel

MOST glorious Virgin, you were chosen by the eternal Counsel to be the Mother of the eternal Word made flesh. You are the treasurer of divine graces and the advocate of sinners. I who am your most unworthy servant have recourse to you. Graciously be my guide and counselor in this valley of tears.

Obtain for me, through the Precious Blood of your divine Son, the forgiveness of my sins, the salvation of my soul, and the means necessary to obtain it. In like manner, obtain for holy Church victory over her enemies and the spread of Jesus' kingdom over the whole earth.

Prayer to Our Lady of Guadalupe

OUR Lady of Guadalupe, mystical rose, intercede for the Church, protect the Holy Father, help all who invoke you in their necessities. Since you are the ever Virgin Mary and Mother of the true God, obtain for us from your most holy Son the grace of a firm and a sure hope amid the bitterness of life, as well as an ardent love and the precious gift of final perseverance.

Our Lady, Help of Christians

MARY, powerful Virgin, you are the mighty and glorious protector of the Church. You are the marvelous help of Christians. You are awe-inspiring as an army in battle array. In the midst of our anguish, struggle, and distress, defend us from the power of the enemy, and at the hour of our death receive our soul in heaven.

Our Lady of Lourdes

O IMMACULATE Virgin Mary, you are the refuge of sinners, the health of the sick, and the comfort of the afflicted. By your appearances at the Grotto of Lourdes you made it a privileged sanctuary where your favors are given to people streaming to it from the whole world. Over the years countless sufferers have obtained the cure of their infirmities—whether of soul, mind, or body. Therefore I come with limitless confidence to implore your motherly intercession.

The Coin of Tribute — " 'Show Me the coin that is used for the tax.' . . . They brought Him a denarius. . . . 'Give to Caesar what is due to Caesar, and to God what is due to God' " — *Mt 22:19ff.*

Jesus Institutes the Holy Eucharist — Jesus "took bread and after giving thanks, He broke it and gave it to them, saying, 'This is My Body. . . . Do this in memory of Me.' " — *Lk 22:19.*

The Agony in the Garden — "After withdrawing from them . . . [Jesus] knelt down and prayed. . . . Then an angel from heaven appeared to Him and gave Him strength" — *Lk 22:41ff.*

The Scourging and Crowning — "Pilate ordered that Jesus be scourged. After this, the soldiers twisted some thorns into a crown and placed it on His head." — *Jn 19:1f.*

THE HOLY ROSARY

The devotion of the holy Rosary has been treasured in the Church for centuries. It is a summary of Christian faith in language and prayers inspired by the Bible. It calls to mind the most important events in the lives of Jesus and Mary. These events are called Mysteries and are divided into four groups of decades. They are: the five Joyful, the five Luminous, the five Sorrowful, and the five Glorious Mysteries. Each decade consists of one "Our Father," ten "Hail Marys," and one "Glory be to the Father."

How to Say the Rosary

1. *Begin on the crucifix and say the Apostles' Creed.*
2. *On the 1st bead, say 1 Our Father.*
3. *On the next 3 beads, say Hail Mary.*
4. *Next say 1 Glory Be. Then announce and think of the first Mystery and what it means, and say 1 Our Father.*
5. *Say 10 Hail Marys and 1 Glory Be to the Father.*
6. *Announce the second Mystery and continue in the same way until each of the five Mysteries of the selected group or decades is said.*

THE FIVE JOYFUL MYSTERIES

(Said on Mondays and Saturdays, and Sundays from Advent until Lent)

The Joyful Mysteries *direct our mind to the Son of God, Jesus Christ, our Lord and Savior, Who took human nature from a human mother, Mary. They also bring to our attention some of the extraordinary events that preceded, accompanied, and followed Christ's Birth.*

1. The Annunciation

Mary, you received with deep humility the news of the Angel Gabriel that you were to be the Mother of God's Son; obtain for me a similar *humility.*

Lk 1:26-38; Isa 7:10-15

2. The Visitation

Mary, you showed true charity in visiting Elizabeth and remaining with her for three months before the birth of John the Baptist; obtain for me the grace to *love my neighbor.*

Lk 1:39-56

3. The Birth of Jesus

Jesus, You accepted poverty when You were placed in the manger although You were our God; grant that I may have the *spirit of poverty.*

Lk 2:1-14; Mt 2:1-12; Gal 4:1-7

4. The Presentation in the Temple

Mary, you obeyed the law of God in presenting the Child Jesus in the Temple; obtain for me the *virtue of obedience.*

Lk 2:22-40

5. The Finding in the Temple

Mary, you were sad at the loss of Jesus and joyous on finding Him surrounded by teachers in the Temple; obtain for me the *virtue of piety.*

Lk 2:42-52

THE FIVE LUMINOUS MYSTERIES*

(Said on Thursdays [except during Lent])

The Luminous Mysteries *recall to our mind important events of the Public Ministry of Christ through which He announces the coming of the Kingdom of God.*

1. Christ's Baptism in the Jordan

Mt 3:13-17; Isa 42:1-2, 4-5

Jesus, at Your Baptism the Father called You His beloved Son and the Holy Spirit came upon You to invest You with Your mission; help me to *keep my Baptismal Promises.*

2. Christ's Self-Manifestation at Cana

Jn 2:1-11

Mary, the first among believers in Christ, upon your intercession your Son changed water into wine and brought the disciples to faith; help me to *do whatever Jesus says.*

---

* Added to the Mysteries of the Rosary by Pope John Paul II in his Apostolic Letter of October 16, 2002, entitled *The Rosary of the Virgin Mary.* They are reprinted here from our book *Pray the Rosary,* which in 2002 received the Imprimatur from Most Rev. Frank J. Rodimer, Bishop of Paterson.

3. Christ's Proclamation of the Kingdom

Mk 1:14-15; Mt 5:1-12

Jesus, You preached the Kingdom of God with its call to forgiveness, inaugurating the ministry of mercy; help me to *seek forgiveness for my sins.*

4. The Transfiguration of Our Lord

Mt 17:1-8; Mk 9:2-8; Lk 9:28-36

Jesus, the glory of the Godhead shone forth from Your face as the Father commanded the Apostles to be transfigured by the Spirit; help me to *be a new person in You.*

5. Christ's Institution of the Eucharist

Mt 26:26-30; 1 Cor 11:23-25

Jesus, at the Last Supper, You offered Your Body and Blood as food under the signs of bread and wine and testified to Your love for humanity; help me to *attain active participation at Mass.*

THE FIVE SORROWFUL MYSTERIES

(Said on Tuesdays and Fridays throughout the year, and daily from Ash Wednesday until Easter Sunday)

The Sorrowful Mysteries *recall to our mind the mysterious events surrounding Christ's sacrifice of His life so that sinful humanity might be reconciled with God.*

1. The Agony in the Garden

Mt 26:36-40

Jesus, in the Garden of Gethsemane, You suffered a bitter agony because of our sins; grant me *true contrition.*

2. The Scourging at the Pillar

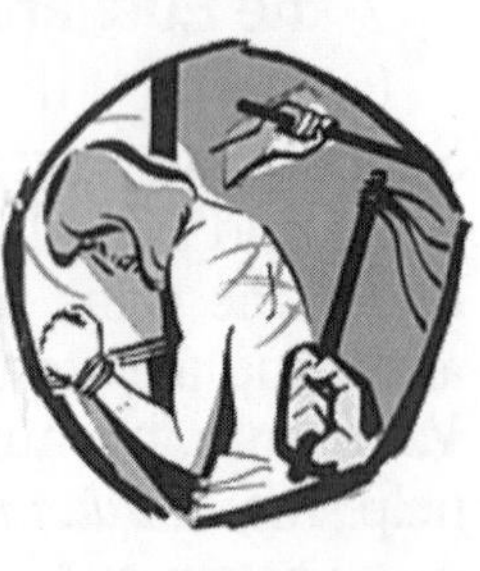

Mt 27:26

Jesus, You endured a cruel scourging and Your flesh was torn by heavy blows; help me to have the *virtue of purity.*

3. The Crowning with Thorns

Mt 27:27-31

Jesus, You patiently endured the pain from the crown of sharp thorns that was forced upon Your head; grant me the strength to have *moral courage.*

4. The Carrying of the Cross

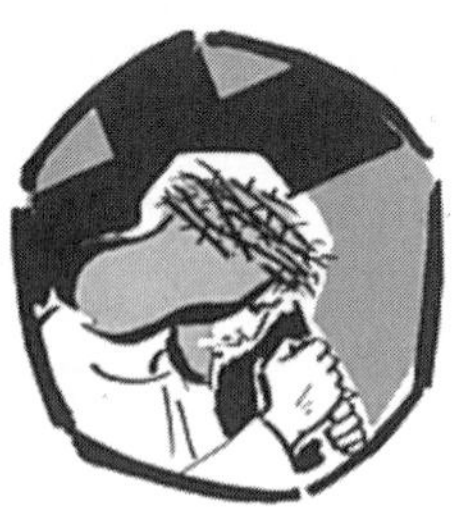

Mt 27:32

Jesus, You willingly carried your Cross for love of Your Father and all people; grant me the *virtue of patience.*

5. The Crucifixion

Mt 27:33-35; Jn 19:31-37

Jesus, for love of me You endured three hours of torture on the Cross and gave up Your Spirit; grant me the grace of *final perseverance.*

THE FIVE GLORIOUS MYSTERIES

(Said on Wednesdays [except during Lent] and the Sundays from Easter until Advent)

The Glorious Mysteries *recall to our mind the ratification of Christ's sacrifice for the redemption of the world, and our sharing in the fruits of His sacrifice.*

1. The Resurrection

Jesus, You rose from the dead in triumph and remained for forty days with your disciples, instructing and encouraging them; increase my *faith.*

Mk 16:1-7; Jn 20:19-31

2. The Ascension

Jesus, in the presence of Mary and the disciples You ascended to heaven to sit at the Father's right hand; increase the *virtue of hope* in me.

Mk 16:14-20; Acts 1:1-11

3. The Descent of the Holy Spirit

Jesus, as You promised, You sent the Holy Spirit upon Mary and the disciples under the form of tongues of fire; increase my *love for God.*

Jn 14:23-31; Acts 2:1-11

4. The Assumption

Mary, by the power of God you were assumed into heaven and united with your Divine Son; help me to have *true devotion* to you.

Lk 1:41-50; Ps 45; Gen 3:15

5. The Crowning of the Blessed Virgin

Mary, you were crowned Queen of heaven by your Divine Son to the great joy of all the Saints; obtain *eternal happiness* for me.

Rev 12:1; Jud 13:18-20; 15:9-10

Prayer after the Rosary

O GOD, Whose only-begotten Son, by His Life, Death, and Resurrection, has purchased for us the rewards of eternal life: grant, we beseech You, that, meditating upon these mysteries of the Most Holy Rosary of the Blessed Virgin Mary, we may imitate what they contain and obtain what they promise, through the same Christ our Lord.

Litany of the Blessed Virgin Mary

LORD, have mercy. *Christ, have mercy.*
Lord, have mercy.
Christ, hear us.
Christ, graciously hear us.
God, the Father of heaven, *have mercy on us.*
God the Son, Redeemer of the world, *have mercy on us.*
God the Holy Spirit,*
Holy Trinity, one God,*
Holy Mary, *pray for us.***
Holy Mother of God,

***** *"Have mercy on us" is repeated here.*

**** *"Pray for us" is repeated after each invocation.*

Holy Virgin of virgins,
Mother of Christ,
Mother of the Church,
Mother of divine grace,
Mother most pure,
Mother most chaste,
Mother inviolate,
Mother undefiled,
Mother most amiable,
Mother most admirable,
Mother of good counsel,
Mother of our Creator,
Mother of our Savior,
Virgin most prudent,
Virgin most venerable,
Virgin most renowned,
Virgin most powerful,
Virgin most merciful,
Virgin most faithful,
Mirror of justice,
Seat of wisdom,
Cause of our joy,
Spiritual vessel,
Vessel of honor,
Singular vessel of devotion,
Mystical rose,
Tower of David,
Tower of ivory,
House of gold,
Ark of the covenant,
Gate of heaven,
Morning star,
Health of the sick,
Refuge of sinners,
Comforter of the afflicted,
Help of Christians,
Queen of angels,
Queen of patriarchs,
Queen of prophets,
Queen of apostles,
Queen of martyrs,
Queen of confessors,
Queen of virgins,
Queen of all saints,
Queen conceived without original sin,
Queen assumed into heaven,

Queen of the most holy Rosary,
Queen of families,
Queen of peace,

Lamb of God, You take away the sins of the world; *spare us, O Lord!*

Lamb of God, You take away the sins of the world; *graciously hear us, O Lord!*

Lamb of God, You take away the sins of the world; *have mercy on us.*

℣. Pray for us, O holy Mother of God.

℟. *That we may be made worthy of the promises of Christ.*

LET us pray. Grant, we beg You, O Lord God, that we Your servants may enjoy lasting health of mind and body, and by the glorious intercession of the Blessed Mary, ever Virgin, be delivered from present sorrow and enter into the joy of eternal happiness. Through Christ our Lord. ℟. *Amen.*

Rosary Novena Prayer

HOLY Virgin Mary, Mother of God and our Mother, accept this Holy Rosary which I offer you to show my love for you and my firm confidence in your powerful intercession. I offer it as an act of faith in the mysteries of the Incarnation and the Redemption, as an act of thanksgiving to God for all His love for me and all mankind, as an act of atonement for the sins of the world, especially my own, and as an act of petition to God through your intercession for all the needs of God's people on earth, but especially for this earnest request. *(Mention your request.)*

I beg you, dear Mother of God, present my petition to Jesus, your

Son. I know that you want me to seek God's will in my request. If what I ask for should not be God's will, pray that I may receive that which will be of greater benefit for my soul. I put all my confidence in you.

THE FIVE FIRST SATURDAYS IN HONOR OF THE IMMACULATE HEART OF MARY

The observance of the First Saturday in honor of the Immaculate Heart of Mary is intended to console her Immaculate Heart, and to make reparation to it for all the blasphemies and ingratitude of men.

This devotion and the wonderful promises connected with it were revealed by the Blessed Virgin with these words recorded by Lucy, one of the three children to whom the Blessed Virgin appeared at Fatima, Portugal, in 1917:

I promise to help at the hour of death, with the graces needed for salvation, whoever on the First Saturday of five consecutive months shall:

1. *Confess and receive Holy Communion.*
2. *Recite five decades of the Rosary.*
3. *And keep me company for [fifteen] minutes while meditating on the [twenty] Mysteries of the Rosary, with the intention of making reparation to me.*

Act of Reparation

O MOST holy Virgin and our Mother, we listen with grief to the complaints of your Immaculate Heart surrounded with the thorns placed therein at every moment by the blasphemies and ingratitude of ungrateful humanity. We are moved by the ardent desire of loving you as our Mother and of promoting a true devotion to your Immaculate Heart.

We therefore kneel before you to manifest the sorrow we feel for the grievances that people cause you, and to atone by our prayers and sacrifices for the offenses with which they return your love. Obtain for them and for us the pardon of so many sins. Hasten the conversion of sinners that they may love Jesus and cease to offend the Lord, already so much offended. Turn your eyes of mercy toward us, that we may love God with all our heart on earth and enjoy Him forever in heaven.

"All you . . . Saints of God, make intercession for us."

PRAYERS TO VARIOUS SAINTS

The Saints are our friends living now with God. They passed through the same journey of life as we do and have reached the glory of heaven. They are bathed in God's light and intercede for us.

By our devotion to the Saints, we seek from them "example in their way of life, fellowship in their communion, and aid by their intercession" (Vatican II).

The following prayers to the Saints will help us to worship God and also to ask the prayers of the Saints to obtain the graces we need through our Lord Jesus Christ.

Prayer to St. Joseph

O GLORIOUS St. Joseph, you were chosen by God to be

the foster father of Jesus, the most pure spouse of Mary, ever Virgin, and the head of the Holy Family. You have been chosen by Christ's Vicar as the heavenly Patron and Protector of the Church founded by Christ.

Protect the Sovereign Pontiff and all bishops and priests united with him. Be the protector of all who labor for souls amid the trials and tribulations of this life; and grant that all peoples of the world may follow Christ and the Church He founded.

Dear St. Joseph, accept the offering I make to you. Be my father, protector, and guide in the way of salvation. Obtain for me purity of heart and a love for the spiritual life.

After your example, let all my actions be directed to the greater glory of God, in union with the Divine Heart of Jesus, the Immaculate Heart of Mary, and your own paternal heart. Finally, pray for me that I may share in the peace and joy of your holy death.

Prayer to St. Joseph for a Happy Death

O BLESSED Joseph, you gave forth your last breath in the loving embrace of Jesus and Mary. When the seal of death shall close my life, come with Jesus and Mary to aid me. Obtain for me this solace for that hour—to die with their holy arms around me. Jesus, Mary, Joseph, I commend my soul, living and dying, into your sacred arms.

Prayer to St. Michael the Archangel

Patron of the Sick

ST. Michael the Archangel, defend us in the day of battle; be our safeguard against the wiles and wickedness of the devil. May God rebuke him, we humbly pray, and do thou, O prince of the heavenly host, by the power of God cast into hell Satan and all the other evil spirits, who prowl through the world, seeking the ruin of souls.

Prayer to One's Guardian Angel

Daily Protector throughout Life

DEAR Angel, in His goodness God gave you to me to guide, protect, and enlighten me, and to bring me back to the right way when I go astray. Encourage me when I am disheartened, and instruct me when I err in my judgment. Help me to become more Christlike, and so some day to be accepted into the company of Angels and Saints in heaven.

Prayer to St. Ann

Patroness of Homemakers

DEAR Saint, we know nothing about you except your name. But you gave us the Mother of God who called herself handmaid of the Lord. In your home you raised the Queen of Heaven and are rightly the model of homemakers. In your womb came to dwell the new Eve uniquely conceived without sin. Intercede for us that we too may remain free from sin.

Prayer to St. Monica

Patroness of Mothers

EXEMPLARY Mother of the great Augustine, you perseveringly pursued your wayward son with love and affection and pardon and counsel and powerful cries to heaven. Intercede for all mothers in our day so that they may learn to draw their children to God. Teach them how to remain close to their children, even the prodigal sons and daughters who have sadly gone astray.

Prayer to St. Theresa of the Child Jesus

Patroness of Missionaries

DEAR Little Flower of Lisieux, how wonderful was the short life you led. Though cloistered, you went far and wide through fervent prayers and great sufferings. You obtained from God untold helps and graces for his evangelists. Help all missionaries in their work and teach all of us to spread Christianity in our own neighborhoods and family circles.

Prayer to St. Christopher

Patron of Motorists

DEAR Saint, you have inherited a beautiful name — Christopher — as a result of a wonderful legend that while carrying people across a raging stream you also carried the Child Jesus. Teach us to be true Christ-bearers to those who do not know Him. Protect all drivers who often transport those who bear Christ within them.

Prayer to St. Francis of Assisi

Patron of Catholic Action

DEAR Saint, once worldly and vain, you became humble and poor for the sake of Jesus and had an extraordinary love for the Crucified, which showed itself in your body by the imprints of Christ's Sacred Wounds.

In our selfish and sensual age, how greatly we need your secret that draws countless men and women to imitate you. Teach us also great love for the poor and unswerving loyalty to the Vicar of Christ.

Prayer to St. Jude

Patron of Desperate Causes

ST. Jude, apostle of Christ, the Church honors and prays to you universally as the patron of hopeless and difficult cases. Pray for us in our needs. Make use, we implore you, of this powerful privilege given to you to bring visible and speedy help where help is needed. Pray that we humbly accept the trials and disappointments and mistakes which are a part of our human nature.

Let us see the reflection of the sufferings of Christ in our daily trials and tribulations. Let us see in a spirit of great faith and hope the part we even now share in the joy of Christ's resurrection, and which we long to share fully in heaven. Intercede that we may again experience this joy in answer to our present needs if it is God's desire for us. *(Here make your request.)*

We know our prayers will be heard through your intercession.

Prayer to St. Anthony

Patron of Motorists

O HOLY St. Anthony, gentlest of Saints, your love for God and charity for His creatures made you worthy even on earth to possess miraculous powers. Miracles waited on your word which you were ever ready to speak for those in trouble or anxiety. Encouraged by this thought, I implore you to obtain for me my request *(here mention your intention)*.

The answer to my prayer may require a miracle; even so, you are the Saint of miracles. O gentle and loving St. Anthony, whose heart is ever full of human sympathy, whisper my petition into the ears of the sweet Infant Jesus, Who loved to be enfolded in your arms, and the gratitude of my heart will be ever yours.

Prayer to St. Rita

Patroness of Impossible Cases

HOLY Patroness of those in need, St. Rita, your pleadings before your divine Lord are irresistible. For your lavishness in granting favors you have been called the "Advocate of the Hopeless" and even of the "Impossible." You are so humble, so mortified, so patient, and so compassionate in love for your crucified Jesus that you can obtain from Him anything you ask if it is

His Holy Will. Therefore, all confidently have recourse to you in the hope of comfort or relief.

Be propitious toward your suppliants and show your power with God in their behalf. Be generous with your favors now as you have been in so many wonderful cases for the greater glory of God, the spread of your devotion, and the consolation of those who trust in you.

We promise, if our petition is granted, to glorify you by making known your favor, and to bless you and sing your praises. Relying then on your merits and power before the Sacred Heart of Jesus, we ask of you *(here mention your request)*.

Prayer to St. Francis Xavier

Patron of Foreign Missions

O VERY dear St. Francis Xavier, full of divine charity, with you I reverently adore the divine Majesty. Since I greatly rejoice in the singular gifts of grace that the Lord conferred on you in this life, and of glory after death, I return most heartfelt thanks to him, and I beg you to obtain for me, by your powerful intercession, above all the grace to love God well. I also ask you to gain for me (*here insert your petition*).

But if that which I suppliantly ask of you is not for the greater good of my soul, I beg you to obtain for me whatever will better promote both these ends.

Prayer to St. Lucy

Patroness of the Blind

DEAR holy Virgin and Martyr, whom the Church recalls in Eucharistic Prayer I, you valiantly rejected great promises and resisted several threats in remaining faithful to your beloved Lord.

For centuries Christians have invoked you particularly when suffering from eye-trouble. So now we implore your assistance on behalf of *N*. . . . We also ask you to teach us to imitate you and to avoid spiritual blindness of any kind.

Prayer to St. Vincent De Paul

Patron of Charitable Societies

O GOD, You gave St. Vincent de Paul apostolic virtues for

the salvation of the poor and the formation of the clergy. Grant that, endowed with the same spirit, we may love what he loved and act according to his teaching.

Prayer to St. Patrick

Patron of Ireland

DEAR St. Patrick, in your humility you called yourself a sinner, but you became a most successful missionary and prompted countless pagans to follow the Savior. Many of their descendants in turn spread the Good News in numerous foreign lands.

Through your powerful intercession with God, obtain for us the missionaries we need to continue the work you began.

PRAYER FOR VARIOUS NEEDS

Prayer for Cities

CITIES are for needs and wants, divine Father, that cannot be met in isolation. Have we expected from them too much and put in too little? Spur us to renew our cities as You renew the earth in spring, that families may have decent living space, that the poor may have hope fulfilled, that the sick and aged may be treated as persons. May our cities be filled with love, truly homes and not merely structures. Amen.

The Christophers

Prayer for All People

O LORD, we bring before You the distress and dangers of peoples and nations, the pleas of the imprisoned and the captive, the sorrows of the grief-stricken, the needs of the refugees, the impotence of the weak, the weariness of the despondent, and the weaknesses of the aging. O Lord, stay close to all of them.

Prayer for Christ's Mercy

O LORD, show Your mercy to me, and gladden my heart. I am like the man on the way to Jericho who was overtaken by robbers, wounded, and left half-dead: O Good Samaritan, come to my aid. I am like the sheep that went astray: O Good Shepherd, seek me out and bring me home in accord with Your will. Let me dwell in Your house all the days of my life and praise You for ever and ever with those who are there.

Prayer for Friends

LORD Jesus Christ, while on earth You had close and devoted friends, such as John, Lazarus, Martha, and Mary. You showed in this way that friendship is one of life's greatest blessings. Thank You for the friends that You have given me to love me in spite of my failures and weaknesses, and to enrich my life after Your example. Let me ever behave toward them as You behaved toward Your friends. Bind us close together in You and enable us to help one another on our earthly journey.

Prayer for Those Who Study or Teach Christian Doctrine

LORD Jesus Christ, by Your Holy Spirit You give to some the word of wisdom, to others the word of knowledge, and to still others the word of faith. Grant us a knowledge of the Father and of Yourself. Help us to cling steadfastly to the Catholic faith. In our studies and in our teaching make us seek only the extension of Your kingdom and Your holy Church both in ourselves and in others.

Prayer for Priestly or Religious Vocations

O LORD, send workers for Your harvest, so that the

precepts of Your only-begotten Son may always be obeyed and His sacrifice be everywhere renewed. Look with favor upon Your family, and ever increase its numbers. Enable it to lead its sons and daughters to the holiness to which they are called and to work for the salvation of others. Through Christ our Lord.

Prayer for All Church Leaders

LORD Jesus Christ, watch over those who are leaders in Your Church. Keep them faithful to their vocation and to the proclamation of Your message. Strengthen them with the gifts of the Spirit and help them to serve Your people, especially the poor and lowly. Give them a vivid sense of Your presence in the world and a knowledge of how to show it to others.

Prayer for Priests

ALMIGHTY Father, grant to these servants of Yours the dignity of the priesthood. Renew within them the Spirit of holiness. As co-workers with the order of bishops may they be faithful to the ministry that they receive from You, Lord God, and be to others a model of right conduct.

May they be faithful in spreading the good news, so that the words of the Gospel may reach the ends of the earth, and the family of nations, made one in Christ, may become God's one, holy people.

Prayer for Missionaries

LORD Jesus Christ, watch over Your missionaries—priests, religious, and lay people—who leave everything to give testimony to Your Word and Your love. In difficult moments sustain their energies, comfort their hearts, and crown their work with spiritual achievements. Let the adorable image of You crucified on the Cross, which accompanies them throughout life, speak to them of heroism, generosity, love, and peace.

Prayer for the Unity of the Church

HEAVENLY Father, Your blessed Son asked that His Church be one as You and He are one, but Christians have not been united as He prayed. We have isolated ourselves from each other and failed to listen to each other. We have misunderstood and ridiculed and even gone so far as to attack each other. In so doing we have offended against You, against all our brothers and sisters in the Church, and against all who have not believed in You because of our scandalous disunity. Forgive us, Father, and make us fully one. Blot out our sins, renew our minds, enkindle our hearts, and guide us by Your Holy Spirit into that oneness which is Your will.

Prayer to Achieve Inner Peace

SLOW me down, Lord. Ease the pounding of my heart by the quieting of my mind. Steady my hurried pace with a vision of the eternal reach of time. Give me, amid the confusion of the day, the calmness of the everlasting hills. Break the tensions of my nerves and muscles with the soothing music of the singing streams that live in memory.

Help me to know the magical, restoring power of sleep. Teach me the art of taking minute vacations—of slowing down to look at a flower, to chat with a friend, to pat a dog, to read a few lines from a good book.

Slow me down, Lord.

Prayer for Acceptance of God's Holy Will

DEAR God, I know that You love me because You died on the Cross for me. I know that You want nothing for me but the best in the light of eternity. So I trust in Your infinite wisdom and goodness and ask You to grant my request if it is according to Your holy will. I accept whatever You decide. I leave everything up to Your divine goodness and loving care. You are my God.

Prayer for the Family

LORD God, from You every family in heaven and on earth takes its name.

Father, you are Love and Life.

Through Your Son, Jesus Christ, born of woman, and through the Holy Spirit, fountain of divine charity, grant that every family on earth may become for each successive generation a true shrine of life and love.

Grant that Your grace may guide the thoughts and actions of

husbands and wives for the good of their families and of all the families in the world.

Grant that the young may find in the family solid support for their human dignity and for their growth in truth and love.

Grant that love, strengthened by the Sacrament of marriage, may prove mightier than all the weaknesses and trials through which our families sometimes pass.

Through the intercession of the Holy Family of Nazareth, grant that the Church may fruitfully carry out her worldwide mission in and through the family.

Through Christ our Lord, Who is the Way, the Truth and the Life for ever and ever. Amen.

Pope John Paul II

Prayer of the Aging

MAY Christ keep me ever young "to the greater glory of God." For old age comes from Him, old age leads to Him, and old age will touch me only insofar as He wills. To be "young" means to be hopeful, energetic, and smiling. May I accept death in whatever guise it may come to me in Christ, that is, within the process of the development of life.

A smile (inward and outward) means facing with mildness and gentleness whatever befalls me.

Jesus, grant me to serve You, to proclaim You, to glorify You, and to manifest You, to the very end through all the time that remains to me of life, and above all through my death.

Lord Jesus, I commit to Your care my last years, and my death; do not let them impair or spoil the work I have so dreamed of achieving for You.

Prayer for International Organizations

HEAVENLY Father, You created this vast and wonderful universe, redeemed it in the Blood of Your Son, and now guide it by Your Holy Spirit. It is Your will that we live as brothers and sisters, building up the world by the marvelous powers that You have graciously given us.

Look graciously on the representatives of the nations who are gathered together today for the good of all. Enlighten them to put forth wise proposals in accord with Your will. Teach them to deliberate with honesty and with genuine respect for one another. Help them to make just decisions that will redound to the peace and welfare of all nations.

Prayer for the Hungry

LORD Jesus Christ, You urged us to give You food in Your hunger which is visible to us in the starving faces of other human beings.

Let me realize that there are millions of persons—children of the same God and our brothers and sisters—who are dying of hunger although they do not deserve to do so.

Do not allow me to remain indifferent to their crying need, or to soothe my conscience with the thought that I cannot do anything about this evil. Help me to do something—no matter how small—to alleviate their heart-rending want. Also let me pray regularly that these poor starving people will be rewarded for this terrible suffering they are enduring, and be relieved of it as soon as possible.

Prayer for the Grace to Help Others

LORD, make me an instrument of Your peace. Where there is hatred, let me sow love. Where there is injury, let me sow pardon. Where there is friction, let me sow union. Where there is error, let me sow truth. Where there is doubt, let me sow faith. Where there is despair, let me sow hope.

Where there is darkness, let me sow light. Where there is sadness, let me sow joy.

O Divine Master, grant that I may not so much seek to be consoled as to console, to be understood as to understand, to be loved as to love.

For it is in giving that we receive. It is in pardoning that we are pardoned. It is in dying that we are born to eternal life.

St. Francis of Assisi

Prayer before Departing on a Trip

O GOD, You called Abraham Your servant out of Ur and kept him safe and sound in all his wandering. We humbly ask You to protect us Your servants. Be for us a support when setting out, friendship along the way, a little shade from the sun, a safeguard in time of danger, and a haven in shipwreck.

Bear us up in fatigue, and defend us under attack. Under Your protection, let us fulfill the purpose for our trip and return safe and sound to our home.

Prayer to Work for the Things We Pray For

O LORD, give us a mind that is humble, quiet, peaceable, patient, and charitable, and the inspiration of Your Holy Spirit in all our thoughts, words, and deeds. O Lord, give us a lively faith, a firm hope, a fervent charity, and a love of You.

Take from us all lukewarmness in meditation and dullness in

prayer. Give us fervor and delight in thinking of You, Your grace, and Your tender compassion toward us. Give us, good Lord, the grace to work for the things we pray for.

Prayer for Health, Wisdom, and a Sense of Humor

O LORD, give me a good digestion as well as something to digest.

Give me health of body as well as the sense to keep it healthy. Give me a holy soul, O Lord, which keeps its eyes on beauty and purity, so that it will not be daunted on seeing sin.

Give me a soul that knows nothing of boredom, groans, and sighs. Never let me be overly concerned for this inconstant thing that I call me.

Lord, give me a sense of humor, so that I may take some happiness from this life, and share it with others.

Prayer of Self-Offering to God

TAKE, O Lord, and receive my entire liberty, my memory, my understanding, and my whole will. All that I am and all that I possess You have given me. I surrender it all to You to be disposed of according to Your will. Give me only Your love and Your grace; with these I will be rich enough and will desire nothing more.

Prayer for Fortitude

DEAR Jesus, lay your Wounded Hand
Upon my weary head,
And teach me to have courage
In the paths that I must tread.
Bless me, and bless those whom I love,
And give us grace to see
These crosses bravely borne by us
Will keep us close to Thee.
And if at times a shadow falls
In unexpected ways,
Put Your gentle Hand in mine
And guide me through the days.
So bless my people, one and all,
With Thy protecting grace,
And impart to them Thy Wisdom
Ere they meet Thee face to face.

Prayer for Employment

BLESSED Anthony, our intercessor in times of need, you gave yourself as a tireless worker in the vineyard of the Lord. By our labor we produce the things needed for human life. So our work is honorable and holy and makes perfect the work of God's creation.

Pray that I may find work which enhances my human dignity, draws me closer to God, and makes my life, as was yours, a real service to my fellow men.

Provide for me while I am in this trial of unemployment. I need your help, blessed friend. Come to my aid.

Prayer of the Expectant Mother to Saint Gerard Majella

O GREAT Saint Gerard, beloved servant of Jesus Christ, perfect imitator of thy meek and humble Savior, and devoted Child of the Mother of God: enkindle within my heart one spark of that heavenly fire of charity which glowed in thine and made thee a seraph of love.

O glorious Saint Gerard, because, when falsely accused of crime, thou didst bear, like thy Divine Master, without murmur or complaint, the calumnies of wicked men, thou hast been raised up by God as the Patron and Protector of expectant mothers.

Preserve me from danger and from the excessive pains accompanying childbirth, and shield the child which I now carry, that it may see the light of day and receive the lustral waters of baptism, through Jesus Christ our Lord. Amen. *(Nine Hail Marys)*

Rev. Joseph A. Chapoton, C.SS.R.

Prayer of Complete Trust in God

O LORD, help me to realize that nothing will happen to me today that You and I cannot work out together.

Prayer for the Acceptance of God's Will

O LORD, I do not know what to ask You. You alone know my real needs, and You love me more than I even know how to love. Enable me to discern my true needs which are hidden from me. I ask for neither a cross nor a consolation but simply wait in patience for You. My heart is open to You.

For Your great mercy's sake, come to me and help me. Put Your mark on me and heal me, cast me down and raise me up. I silently adore Your holy will and Your inscrutable ways. I offer myself in sacrifice to You and put all my trust in You. I desire only to do Your will. Teach me how to pray.

PRAYERS IN TIME OF SICKNESS AND DEATH

Sickness and pain have always been a heavy burden for man and an enigma to his understanding. Christians suffer sickness and pain as do all other human beings; yet their faith helps them to understand better the mystery of suffering and to bear their pain more bravely. From Christ's words they know that sickness has meaning and value for their own salvation and for the world's; they also know that Christ loved the sick and that during His life He often looked upon the sick and healed them.

It is part of the plan laid down by God's providence that we should struggle

against all sickness and carefully seek the blessings of good health, so that we can fulfill our role in human society and in the Church. Yet we should always be prepared to fill up what is lacking in Christ's sufferings for the salvation of the world as we look forward to all creation being set free in the glory of the children of God.

Prayer of Resignation in Suffering

MERCIFUL Lord of life, I lift up my heart to You in my suffering and ask for Your comforting help. I know that You would withhold the thorns of this life if I could attain eternal life without them. So I throw myself on Your mercy, resigning myself to this suffering. Grant me the grace to bear it and to offer it in union with Your sufferings. No matter what suffering may come my way, let me trust in You.

Prayer for the Restoration of Health

O SACRED Heart of Jesus, I come to ask You for the gift of restored health that I may serve You more faithfully and love You more sincerely. I want to be well if it is Your will and redounds to Your glory.

If on the other hand it is Your will that my sickness continue, I want to bear it with patience. If in Your divine wisdom I am to be restored to health and strength, I will strive to show my gratitude by a constant and faithful service rendered to You, my loving Savior and Redeemer, and my God.

Prayer to God, the Source of Health

GOD our Father, source of all health, be near those who

suffer in the time of weakness and pain; relieve them of their burden and heal them, if it be Your will.

Give peaceful sleep to those who need rest for soul and body, and be with them in their hours of silence. Bless those who know not what another day will bring.

Make them ready for whatever it may be. Whether they must stand, or sit or be confined, grant them a strong spirit.

Inspire with Your love those who bring healing and care to the suffering. May they bestow Your gifts of health and strength wherever they go. Grant this prayer, through Christ our Lord.

Prayer for the Dead

GOD our Father, Your power brings us to birth, Your providence guides our lives, and by Your command we return to dust.

I pray for the dead, especially for *N.* May those who have been dear to me in life find a place with You in heaven.

Lord, those who die still live in Your presence; their lives change but do not end. I pray in hope for my family, relatives and friends, and for all the dead known to You alone.

In company with Christ Who died and now lives may they rejoice in Your kingdom where all our tears are wiped away. Unite us together again as one family, to sing Your praise forever and ever.

Prayer for Departed Relatives, Friends and Benefactors

HEAVENLY Father, accept my prayer for all those in purgatory for whom I should pray because of ties of family, gratitude, justice, or charity. Have mercy on my relatives, friends, and benefactors as well as those who hold positions of authority, both civil and religious. Admit them all to Your eternal happiness in heaven. Eternal rest grant to them, O Lord. And let perpetual light shine upon them. May they rest in peace.

Prayer for All the Faithful Departed

HEAVENLY Father, I believe that in Your wisdom and

justice You willed to purify all persons who die without having attained the state that they need for all eternity, all who have still to expiate completely the sins committed on earth. I also believe that You have mercifully arranged that this process of purification can be aided by the prayers of the living, especially the Eucharist.

Help me to pray for my brothers and sisters who have departed from this world. May their time of purification be short and they be quickly guided into that holy light promised by our Lord to Abraham and his descendants. I offer You sacrifices and prayers of praise. Accept them for all the souls of the faithful departed and admit them all to heavenly joy.

OUR CATHOLIC FAITH

This section presents truths about God which can be known by human reason unaided by revelation, the Mysteries of our Catholic Faith, and the Commandments of God and His Church. Mysteries are supernatural truths revealed to us by God which our human minds alone cannot fully understand. The Mysteries tell us what we know about God, and the Commandments show us how to love Him.

God and His Attributes

GOD is the Creator and Ruler of the universe. He alone is independent because He alone exists of Himself. All other things have received existence from Him and thus are dependent upon Him.

God is eternal. He has always existed; He has always been and always will be.

God is a pure spirit, a sovereign intelligence who has no body and who cannot be perceived by our senses. Present everywhere, He can penetrate our most secret thoughts; all-powerful, He can do all things. He governs all by His love, His mercy, and His justice, and nothing comes about without His command or without His permission.

God is infinitely good, infinitely holy, infinitely just; in a word, He is infinitely perfect: He possesses without restriction or measure all perfections.

The Holy Trinity

THERE is only one God, but there are in Him three distinct Persons: the Father, the Son, and the Holy Spirit.

The Father is God, the Son is God, the Holy Spirit is God. However, these three persons are not three Gods, but

The Place of the Skull — "They took Jesus away, and carrying the cross by Himself, He went out to what is called the Place of the Skull (in Hebrew, *Golgotha*)." — *Jn 19:16f.*

The Crucifixion and Death of Jesus — "When they came to the place called The Skull, they crucified Jesus there. . . . 'Father, into Your hands I commend My spirit.' And with these words, He breathed His last." *—Lk 23:33, 46.*

The Resurrection of Jesus Christ — "I have risen: I am with You once more; You placed Your hand on me to keep me safe. How great is the depth of Your wisdom, alleluia!" — *Easter Entrance Ant.*

The Ascension of Our Lord Jesus Christ — Jesus "led them out as far as Bethany, and lifting up His hands He blessed them. While He was blessing them, He departed from them, and was taken up to heaven." — *Lk 24:50ff.*

only one God. The Son is the Word, or the interior voice of the Father, and begotten by the Father alone; the Holy Spirit is the mutual Love of the Father and the Son, and He proceeds from both. The three Persons of the Blessed Trinity are equal in all things because they have only one nature, the Divine Nature: in this consists the Mystery of the Holy Trinity.

Creatures of God

AMONG the creatures of God, the most perfect are Angels and men. The Angels are pure spirits created to adore God and execute His commands.

Many of these Angels revolted against their Creator, Who, in turn, condemned them to hell. These Angels whom we call *demons* or *evil spirits* hate God and tempt man on earth to defy the laws of God so as to be condemned to the same tortures that they themselves suffer.

The faithful Angels are confirmed in grace and have their abode in heaven for all eternity. We call some *Guardian Angels* because God has appointed them to keep watch over man on earth. Each one of us has a Guardian Angel.

Adam and Eve

GOD formed man and gave to him a living and immortal soul, created to His own image.

From Adam, the first man, and from Eve, whom God gave to Adam as a companion, has sprung the whole human race.

God has created us to know Him, to love Him, and to serve Him in this world and to be happy with Him forever in heaven.

God not only gave our first parents an immortal soul: He elevated them to a supernatural life of grace; He called them to enjoy His eternal happiness. In this first state of original justice, He exempted them from the ravages of sickness, ignorance, concupiscence, and death.

Original Sin

HAVING been tempted by the devil, our first parents disobeyed God. For this reason they lost for themselves and for their posterity that life of grace and holiness. Adam transmitted that same disgrace and degradation to all his descendants, and this is the state of original sin to which we all are born. The gates of heaven were closed to mankind as a result of original sin.

Only Mary, in view of the merits of her Divine Son, was exempt from original sin—from the first moment of her conception, i.e., from the moment her soul was created and infused into her body it was free from original sin and filled with sanctifying grace. This privilege is called her *Immaculate Conception.*

The Promise of a Redeemer

GOD had pity upon man whom He had created with such love; and having subjected man from the time of

Adam's fall to sickness, ignorance, concupiscence and death, He promised a Redeemer who would make reparation for the sin of Adam and Eve and reopen the gates of heaven.

The human race never did completely forget this divine promise, although for many centuries before the coming of the Redeemer, it languished in the ways of corruption.

The hope for a Redeemer was kept alive among the Hebrew people, through the successive missions which God gave to the Patriarchs, Moses, and the Prophets. These extraordinary men were not raised up for the sole purpose of reminding the Jews of their obligation to the moral law, but also to keep alive their hope and to foretell the character and redeeming works of the future Messiah.

The Coming of the Savior

WHEN the time appointed by the wisdom of God had come, the

Son of God, the Second Person of the Blessed Trinity, became Man in the womb of the Virgin Mary. The Church celebrates the birth of our Blessed Lord Jesus Christ on Christmas Day.

He received the name *Jesus,* meaning *Savior* because He came to save the world. *Christ,* meaning *Anointed One,* was the name given by the Chosen People of God to their Priests, Kings and Prophets by reason of the holy unction with which they were consecrated. This name is eminently adapted to the Son of God made Man Who was anointed not by means of an exterior and material unction but by the fullness of the divinity which resides in Him.

The Incarnation of Jesus

JESUS Christ is the Son of God, equal and consubstantial with the Father in all things. Jesus Christ is Man because He possesses all that which constitutes human nature: a body, and a soul. This union of Divine nature and human nature in Jesus

Christ is called the *Mystery of the Incarnation.* There are, then, in Jesus Christ, two natures and one Person: the Person of the Son of God, and the nature of God and the nature of man.

Jesus Christ—Our Lord and Savior

JESUS Christ came upon earth to destroy the reign of sin. He fought sin by His example, prophecies, and miracles; but above all He triumphed over sin by the merits of His Passion and death.

He delivered Himself up to the malice of His enemies; He allowed Himself to be condemned to cruel punishment and to be crucified. He shed all His Blood while praying for His persecutors: taking the place of the guilty, He suffered and died for them. He made satisfaction for the sins of all human beings: for those who preceded His coming as well as those who followed Him, meriting graces without number and without measure for their sanctification and salvation.

The Redemption

JESUS Christ did not suffer and die as God, for a Divine Nature can neither suffer nor die. He died as Man; but as God, He has given an infinite value to His sufferings and death. He died for all human beings, including those who do not take advantage of His saving merits. The day in which the Church, in a special manner, commemorates the death of Jesus Christ is called Good Friday.

This death of the Son of God made Man, offering His very life on the Cross as a sacrifice for the salvation of humankind, is called the *Mystery of the Redemption* of the human race: a mystery of love in which God has united His mercy and justice, in pardoning sinful human beings in view of the sacrifice and merits of His innocent Son.

Immediately after the death of Jesus Christ, His body was placed in a tomb. He then descended into hell, that is, the place of the dead, to free all the souls of the just, the Patriarchs, and Prophets who were detained there awaiting the coming of the Messiah and the Redemption of the world.

The Resurrection

THE third day after His death, Jesus Christ rose from the dead. This signal of His mission and of His divinity has confirmed His work, and has given us a solid foundation for our Faith and an infallible assurance of our hope. The Church commemorates this great miracle on Easter Sunday.

The Ascension

FORTY days after His Resurrection, Jesus Christ ascended into heaven. The Church commemorates this event on the Feast of the Ascension.

The Primitive Church

JESUS Christ has left upon earth a *Church,* a holy people and society which unites in one body the children of God all over the world. He Himself gathered together the first members, His disciples, from among whom He chose His twelve Apostles. To them especially, He entrusted His mission to teach all nations, to administer the Sacraments, to offer the sacrifice of His Body and Blood, and to govern the Church.

He chose particularly one of them, to whom He gave the name of Peter (the Rock), indicating by this name that He wanted to make him the foundation stone upon which His Church would be built. He appointed Peter Prince of the Apostles, Pastor of Pastors, and designated him to be His Vicar on earth after His Ascension into Heaven. St. Peter, the other Apostles, and the disciples made up the membership of the Church after Jesus ascended into Heaven. The advent of the Holy Spirit fertilized its beginnings and gave the Apostles the gift of prophecy.

The Marks of the True Church

THE chief marks of the Church are four: It is one, holy, catholic or universal, and apostolic.

The Church is *one* because all its members, according to the will of Christ, profess the same faith, have the same Sacrifice and Sacraments, and are united under one and the same visible head, the Pope.

The Church is *holy* through Jesus Christ Who is the source of all holiness: in its doctrine, which is the doctrine of Jesus Christ, of which it is the custodian; in its Sacraments, which the Divine Savior has established to sanctify human beings.

The Church is *catholic,* or universal, i.e., it is not destined for one race, but it will be the light and salvation of all peoples of the world. There is not one country where the good tidings of salvation have not been or should not be announced by her.

The Church is *apostolic,* that is, it had its beginning with the Apostles. In commanding His Apostles to go forth and teach all nations, to call them to His Church, and to let them enter through the door of Baptism, Jesus Christ promised to assist them in their ministry until the consummation of the world. This promise embraces all times, not merely apostolic times, nor does Jesus Christ address Himself personally to the Apostles alone but to all those who would succeed them till the end of the world.

The Apostles have had as their successors Bishops, whom they consecrated and who in turn consecrated others so that the apostolic ministry has never been interrupted. St. Peter, Prince of the Apostles, was the first Bishop of Rome, where he ended his apostolate in glorious martyrdom. His successors in the See of Rome will always preserve the primacy of honor and of jurisdiction which Jesus gave to St. Peter.

In virtue of this succession, the Pope, the Bishop of Rome, is the Vicar of Jesus Christ, the Head of all the Church, the Father of all Christians. To him, in the person of St. Peter, has been given the power to shepherd, to reign, and to rule the universal Church: so that the Pope and all the Bishops in communion with him continually represent on earth the Apostolic college established by our Savior.

By the legitimate succession of its pastors, principally of its Roman Pontiffs, from the Apostles down to our own times, and until the end of the world, the Church can and will always be able to trace its origin to the Apostles and from them to Jesus Christ.

One Flock, One Shepherd

THE Holy Roman Catholic and Apostolic Church is the only flock of which Jesus Christ, the Son of God, is the only Shepherd. To hear the teachings of the Church and to submit oneself to its laws is to hear Jesus Christ and to obey Him. To refuse to submit to the decisions and laws of the Church is to refuse to submit to Jesus Christ. He Himself has expressly said to His Apostles: *He who hears you, hears Me; and he who rejects you, rejects Me; and he who rejects Me, rejects Him Who sent Me.*

One cannot separate oneself from the Church without at the same time rejecting Jesus Christ; for *there is no other name under heaven given to men by which we must be saved.* When one willfully remains outside the true Church there is no hope for salvation.

Infallibility of the Church

JESUS Christ has given to His Church the privilege of *doctrinal infallibility.* The Pope enjoys this infallibility when he speaks *ex cathedra,* that is, when he speaks to all the Church concerning matters of Faith or Morals. He not merely must speak as a private theologian but he must speak with the manifest intention of obligating the universal Church to consent. The general Councils of the Church enjoy the same privilege of infallibility under the same conditions.

The Mystical Body of Christ

THE faithful who make up the Church represent one body, of which Jesus Christ is the Head. In their capacity as members of this Mystical Body, all are called to participate in the merits of its Divine Head; all are united through participation in the same spiritual benefits: faith, the Sacraments, good works, and prayers. This union continues even after death and is called the *Communion of Saints,* which means the union of the faithful on earth, the blessed in heaven, and the souls in Purgatory, with Christ as their Head.

The Saints who are already in heaven pray for us, and we obtain from God, through the merits of Jesus Christ, powerful assistance in order to attain the happiness which they already enjoy. Accordingly, we on earth, who are battling against the enemy of our salvation, can help by our prayers and other good works of mercy those souls who suffer in Purgatory to expiate their faults and discharge their debts to divine justice.

The Last Judgment

AT the end of time, Jesus Christ will again come with great power and majesty to judge all men and to render to each according to each one's works. This general judgment will be a manifestation and confirmation of the particular judgment to which each one of us must submit immediately after death. But before the last judgment, all men will be resurrected with the same bodies they had during life on earth, so that their bodies will share the same reward or punishment as their souls.

God wants also, by this resurrection, to render more complete the triumph of Jesus Christ over death and sin. Impenitent sinners will suffer eternal punishment; the just, on the other hand, will enjoy the vision and possession of God, eternal happiness.

Sanctifying Grace

SANCTIFYING grace is that grace which confers on our souls a new life, that is, a sharing in the life of God.

Our reconciliation with God, which the redemption of Christ has merited for us, finds its accomplishment in sanctifying grace. Through this most precious gift we participate in the divine life; we have the right to be called children of God. This grace is the source of all our supernatural merits and bestows upon us the right of eternal glory.

Actual Grace

OUR Lord has also merited actual graces for us, those interior and supernatural helps given to us according to our needs in doing good and avoiding evil. These helps are of such necessity that without them it is impossible to elicit a good desire or to have a good thought in the order of salvation. Jesus offered Himself for all human beings; His actual graces are given to all but not in the same measure because God is always the master of His gifts.

Just as there is no one from whom the most powerful grace can take away free will, so also there is no one who can complain that the insufficiency of grace reduced him to the necessity of falling into sin. We all have the sum total of graces sufficient for the acquisition of everlasting life, for which all of us have been created.

Prayer Is Necessary

PRAYER is a means as efficacious as it is necessary for obtaining help from God. Our blessed Lord has urged us often to have recourse to it, and has given us the model of a perfect prayer —*The Lord's Prayer.* To this prayer, the Church usually joins the Angelical Salutation, or the *Hail Mary*, so as to render homage to the Blessed Virgin.

Prayer is necessary for salvation, victory over temptation, the practice of virtue, and perseverance in grace. If the proper things are asked for, and the prayer is made with attention, humility, confidence, sincerity, and perseverance, God will certainly grant our petitions. We do not always obtain what we pray for, either because we have not prayed properly or because God sees that what we are asking would not be for our good.

The Liturgy

EACH year through the Liturgy (especially the Mass), the Church makes present for us the Life, Death, and Resurrection of Jesus. In this way, we can encounter our Lord in His Mysteries, give glory to God, and obtain graces for ourselves and the whole world.

Outline of the Church Year

Advent—*Jesus is near.*
Christmas—*Jesus is with us.*
Epiphany—*Jesus shows His glory.*
Ordinary Time—*Jesus gives lessons for His Church.*
Lent—*Jesus suffers and dies for us.*
Easter—*Jesus triumphs over sin and death.*
Easter Time—*Jesus instructs His Apostles.*
Ascension—*Jesus ascends to His heavenly Father.*
Pentecost—*Jesus sends the Holy Spirit.*
Ordinary Time—*The Spirit carries on the work of Jesus through His Church.*

Holy Mass

ON the Cross Jesus offered His Body and Blood to God the Father for us. In the Mass this great act is renewed for our benefit. We offer Jesus to God the Father in adoration, thanksgiving, reparation, and petition. We receive Jesus back from the Father as our Bread for eternal life. We sing hymns to praise God and to show our joy at Mass.

Major Parts of Holy Mass

Introductory Rites—*We speak to God in acts of contrition, praise, and petition.*

Liturgy of the Word—*We listen to what God says to us in the Readings, the Gospel, and the Homily.*

Liturgy of the Eucharist—

- Preparation of the Gifts—*With the priest we present the gifts of bread and wine.*
- Eucharistic Prayer—*At the consecration this bread and wine are changed into the Body and Blood of Jesus.*
- Communion Rite—*We receive Jesus Who has given Himself in love.*

Concluding Rite—*We receive God's blessing and go forth to bring the good news of Jesus to others by word and example.*

The Seven Sacraments

JESUS is present among us today by means of the Sacraments. Through them Jesus acts in His Church and effects the salvation of all human beings. Sacraments are sensible signs, instituted by Christ to give us grace, which makes us children of God and heirs of heaven.

Our natural life follows a series of stages: we are born and grow until we become adults and can live on our own. In instituting the Seven Sacraments Jesus gave us helps to be born and grow to adulthood in the supernatural life—to be with us in every phase of life.

Baptism—*Christ gives us a new life: the life of grace in His Church. We celebrate our birth to faith, as children of God, and we die to sin.*

Confirmation—*Christ strengthens us as Christians and He makes us His soldiers and apostles to defend and spread the faith.*

Eucharist—*We celebrate the Lord's Passover, the sacrifice of the Cross. Christ feeds us with the Bread of Life, His Body and Blood.*

Penance—*Christ forgives our sins and restores or increases our grace. We celebrate our conversion and reconciliation with God and the Church.*

Anointing of the Sick—*Christ strengthens our soul in the face of sickness and death. We celebrate the Christian hope in life eternal.*

Holy Orders—*Christ consecrates His ministers for the Priestly Service of the People of God.*

Matrimony—*Christ sanctifies the indissoluble union of man and woman in mutual love and support, to have children and to bring them up in the Catholic faith.*

The Word of God

GOD *revealed himself* in time. He intervened in history and communicated to human beings His merciful plans. The Bible (Word of God) is the record of this self-revelation of God which was set forth in a *message* as well as in *events.* God spoke and acted—word and event went together.

Human beings left to themselves cannot discover all the mysteries of God or His creatures. In His goodness, God has revealed to us many truths which He wants us to know.

God's Revelation is contained in the Bible and in Sacred Tradition.

The Bible

THE Bible is a collection of sacred books, which were composed under the positive influence of the Holy Spirit by men chosen by God, and which have been accepted by the Church as inspired. It is the most authorized, most admirable, and most important book in the world because it is the only "divine book," the word of God in the language of man.

The two main parts of the Bible are the Old Testament and the New Testament. The word "testament" is used here in the sense of "agreement" or "covenant."

The Old Testament is a record of the *old agreement* between God (Yahweh) and His chosen people, the Hebrews. It describes the remote preparation for the coming of the Messiah.

The New Testament is a record of the *new agreement* made by God with the whole human race through the Life, Death, and Resurrection of Jesus Christ, the Son of God made Man.

Sacred Tradition

SACRED Tradition is the Word of God given to the Apostles by Christ and the Holy Spirit and handed down to their successors through the Church by means of prayer and Creeds, liturgical practices, and authoritative writings (Popes, bishops, and theologians).

Tradition can be defined as the way the Church understands and lives the teachings of Jesus *at any particular mo-*

ment in time. Tradition and Sacred Scripture form one deposit of the Word of God. Thus, Scripture, Tradition, and the Catholic Church combine to bring us God's revelation.

The Catholic Church is the official interpreter of the Bible. As the people of God—both of the Old Covenant *in figure* and of the New Covenant *in reality*—she wrote the Sacred Scriptures. And as the Church of Christians, she has always treasured them.

She encourages her members to study the Scriptures for she knows that "ignorance of the Scriptures is ignorance of Christ."

God's Word to Us Today

WHEN reading the Bible, we should take pains to discover the literal sense of every passage. Reading introductions and footnotes in our Bible is very important in this respect. We should realize that the Bible is God's Word speaking to us today.

God's Law—
The Ten Commandments

Our Duties to God

1. "I am the Lord, your God: you shall not have other gods besides Me." Our main duties to God are embodied in the following Theological Virtues:

a) *Faith* is a virtue by which we firmly believe all that God has revealed and teaches through His Church.

b) *Hope* is a virtue by which we have confidence in God's infinite bounty, His fidelity to His promises, the eternal salvation which should be the ultimate end of all our desires, and the graces which we need to attain everlasting life.

c) *Charity* is a virtue by which we love God above all things for His own sake.

2. "You shall not take the name of the Lord your God in vain." The profound respect which the name of God requires prohibits us from taking His

name in vain, and to utter any false statement against truth or justice. It prohibits also all manner of oaths, imprecations, and blasphemies. Finally, the Second Commandment admonishes us against vows lightly made, and imposes the obligations of fulfilling those already made.

3. "Remember to keep holy the Sabbath Day." Notwithstanding interior worship, we owe to God an exterior and public worship, so as to stir up one another to serve and worship Him and thus mutually edify one another. It is for this reason that God has commanded us to consecrate one day out of each week to Him, and to abstain from servile works. In the Old Law, the day set aside was Saturday, in memory of the creation of the world; in the New Law, the day set aside is Sunday, in memory of our Lord and Savior Jesus Christ and of the Descent of the Holy Spirit on the Apostles on Pentecost Sunday.

Duties to Ourselves and to Our Neighbor

4. "Honor your father and your mother." The principal duties toward our parents are to respect, love, and obey them and to assist them in their needs. This Commandment also regulates the duties of subjects toward superiors and vice versa; in a word, it regulates all our rights and duties within the family circle and in society.

5. "You shall not kill."

6. "You shall not commit adultery."

7. "You shall not steal."

8. "You shall not bear false witness against your neighbor."

9. "You shall not covet your neighbor's wife."

10. "You shall not covet anything that belongs to your neighbor."

Chief Precepts of the Church

1. To keep holy the day of the Lord's Resurrection: to worship God by participating in Mass every Sunday

and holyday of obligation; to avoid those activities that would hinder renewal of soul and body, e.g., needless work and business activities, unnecessary shopping and so on.

2. To lead a sacramental life: to receive Holy Communion frequently and the Sacrament of Reconciliation regularly—minimally, to receive the Sacrament of Reconciliation at least once a year (annual confession is obligatory only if serious sin is involved); minimally also, to receive Holy Communion at least once a year, between the First Sunday of Lent and Trinity Sunday.

3. To study Catholic teaching in preparation for the Sacrament of Confirmation, to be confirmed, and then to continue to study and advance the cause of Christ.

4. To observe the marriage laws of the Church: to give religious training, by example and word, to one's children; to use parish schools and catechetical programs.

5. To strengthen and support the Church: one's own parish community and parish priests, the worldwide Church and the Pope.

6. To do penance, including abstaining from meat and fasting from food on the appointed days.

7. To join in the missionary spirit and apostolate of the Church.

Holy Days of Obligation in the United States

All Sundays of the year

January 1—*Solemnity of Mary, Mother of God*

Ascension of Our Lord *(Forty days after Easter)*

August 15—*Assumption of the Blessed Virgin Mary*

November 1—*All Saints Day*

December 8—*The Immaculate Conception*

December 25—*Christmas Day*

Sin

EVERY violation of the Commandments of God or of the Church is a sin: *mortal sin*, if three conditions are present—a serious matter, sufficient reflection and full consent of the will; *venial sin*, if the law violated concerns matter which is not grave or the offense is committed without sufficient reflection or full consent of the will. Venial sin does not deprive the soul of sanctifying grace.

Mortal sin deprives us of sanctifying grace and brings eternal punishment to the soul, if we pass from this life before confessing this sin and obtaining forgiveness. However, an act of perfect contrition (sorrow for offending a good and loving God) suffices, if one is not able to go to Confession.

Venial sin carries with it temporal punishment. It also weakens the will, thereby making it more difficult to resist temptation to mortal sin.

ISBN 978-0-89942-910-6